# Ponder Picture Prosper

# Ponder Picture Prosper

## A Proven Method for Getting What You Want in Life, Love, and Work

Dear Herrington Family,
Set goals together. Dream
dreams and expect miracles!
May all your hopes and
dreams come true!
Warm regards,
Marsha

MARSHA BARBER CLARK

Lake House Publishing, LLC

Published by Lake House Publishing, LLC
www.ponderpictureprosper.com

Clark, Marsha Barber.

Ponder picture prosper : a proven method for getting what you want in life, love, and work / Marsha Barber Clark. — 1st ed. — Bellaire, Mich. : Lake House Publishing, c2009.

p. ; cm.

ISBN: 978-0-9822108-0-2

1. Goal (Psychology). 2. Motivation (Psychology). 3. Success. 4. Achievement motivation. I. Title.

BF505.G6 C53 2009 2008941166
158.1—dc22 0903

*Printed in the United States of America*
10 9 8 7 6 5 4 3 2 1

Cover photos by: Charles L. Clark

*Interior and cover design by To The Point Solutions*
*www.tothepointsolutions.com*

*To Chuck, Brendan, and Shane—*

*who have enriched my life, shared travel adventures, and*

*together, followed our dreams. I love you.*

# Contents

# Acknowledgments

I am most grateful to my parents, Barney and Lorena Barber, for encouraging me to dream and to set goals, even when they seemed outside the realm of possibility. I am forever changed because they allowed me to follow my own path and did not discourage my goals.

I am grateful to my grandmother Gertie Barber, who was a trailblazer for women and who chose a path that few women walked. I thank her for encouraging me to find my own way.

I am eternally grateful to my husband, Chuck Clark, who has always shared his strength with me, especially when I became weary while pursuing my goals. He has been steadfast in his encouragement and love as I worked to complete this book. I love and thank him for helping me through the many facets of publishing and for his insightful contributions.

I love and thank my children, Brendan and Shane, who have read this manuscript and offered their love, encouragement, and incisive observations.

I am forever indebted to my sister, Terri Franzen, for listening to my endless ideas and offering suggestions for completing this project.

I want to thank Mary Jo Zazueta of To The Point Solutions for her expert editing and design skills. Without her guidance, publishing this book would not have been possible.

I want to thank my many friends—Shirley Kratt, Tracy Kiersey, Sue Soderberg, Kimberly Neibauer, Brian Molitor, and Martha Mumma—who offered encouragement and support throughout this journey.

And thank you to the following individuals for their help: Donna Schwartz; Robin Pinkham; Maggie Bethel; Celeste Sturdevant Reed, PhD; George Bearup; Pam Sievers; Shari Baker; Marsha Smith; Tom Emling; Dick Evans; Sr. Helen Huellmantel; Doris Wetters, PhD; Melissa Whitman; and Jaclyn Libowitz.

# Introduction

Since 1987, I have kept a Goal Book. As a result, I have realized many successes. For example, my family and I have traveled across the globe. We lived our lives believing that travel is the University of the World and my husband and I wanted to teach our children history, geography, and sociology through experiential learning. We embraced the quote by Saint Augustine: "The World is a book, and those who do not travel read only a page."

My family has walked on the Great Wall of China, a bridge over the River Kwai, and the smooth stones of the Acropolis. We've seen vibrant-colored fish dart about the Great Barrier Reef and felt the breath of a thousand wildebeests and zebras in their great migration into Kenya. We've gazed at Michelangelo's *Creation of Man* on the ceiling of the Sistine Chapel and touched the flowered walls of the Taj Mahal. We've felt the presence of the ancient Incas in Machu Picchu and stood in the shadow of Stonehenge. We've explored the depths of a pyramid and ridden camels in the Sahara. And, we've made friends with people who shared no common language with us.

Our souls have been touched and we will never be the same.

Because my family has been able to travel to these and other places, people think we've won the lottery. We haven't. When they ask how we do it, the answer is always the same: **we set goals and expect them to happen**. We pondered, pictured, and prospered when the universe arranged the details. We also maintain the attitude that our dreams will be achieved.

The purpose of this book is to inspire you to create a Goal Book for yourself (and your family) so you, too, can live a more satisfying life. I will take you step-by-step through the process of creating a Goal Book that represents everything you want your life to be.

Your task is to determine what you want in life. It is the job of the universe to figure out how to orchestrate the achievement of your goals. The comfort in having a Goal Book is that you can make a list of your goals, express the goals in pictures, plan and prepare for them, and then relax while you wait for the universe to work out the details.

I find that I am a freer and happier person because I don't worry whether or not I'll reach my goals. I realize my goals will come, if not today, then perhaps tomorrow. You, too, can experience this.

I will help you discover your goals. We'll discuss the types of goals that need to be included in your Goal Book, where goals come from, fears you may have in setting goals, considerations in setting marriage and family goals, and general concerns about goal setting.

This book won't take long to read, so you can soon start to create your own Goal Book.

# Ponder Picture Prosper

# ONE

# What Is a Goal Book?

I have had written goals since I was a child. I continued this into adulthood. I found that writing goals and looking at them often was a helpful tool—but nothing as powerful as when my family created a Goal Book.

Our Goal Book contains pictures and clarifying words that illustrate our goals. My husband and I started making a list of places we wanted to take our two sons. We looked at travel brochures and magazines and cut out pictures and glued them on pages so we would remember the sights we wanted to see when we went on a particular trip. We had many adventures planned.

Magical things started to happen. Every year, one or more of the trips came to us in some way. So, we decided to put pages in our Goal Book representing other aspects of our lives. We made pages for changes we wanted to make to our home. We made lists of remodeling projects. We cut out pictures from magazines of bookshelves, closets, porches, and kitchens that represented visions of what we liked. We created pages for the various rooms so we would remember the ideas that appealed to us. When we talked to the designer and builder we showed them the pages so they could see our vision and more accurately design and build what we had in mind.

Then, we created pictures of our other written goals. We talked as a couple about what was important for our family and what achievements we wanted. As our boys grew older, we included them in the family goal setting and we created pages together.

We have found that goals don't have to be in any particular order within the Goal Book. We did start our family Goal Book with our *core* goals (see Chapter 3), including goals for health, happiness, love, and safety. We followed these pages with pictures that represented a happy marriage and family. Our reasoning was that without good health and a happy family life, not much else mattered.

Other pages represented what we felt was most essential to our lives, such as basic needs. We had pages for doing well in school and work and for family togetherness, and pictures representing my husband and me remaining married and growing old together.

Then, we pondered our dreams. We added trips to every location we all agreed on, improvements to our home and yard, cars, and enough money to fund these goals. Each of us also made individual pages that were in concert with the good of the family, such as job changes; individual work goals; and, as parents, we had goals for our children that involved our accountability. This included my husband and me helping them with homework, educating them in areas where the school did not, providing them with good nutrition habits and table manners, providing education through travel experiences, having them go to college, and having enough money to pay for college.

We have had tremendous success reaching our goals and realizing our dreams. Our photo albums now look much like the pages in our Goal Book.

I manage my life and we manage our marriage and family with a Goal Book. We know what we want and what is best for us. We knew our children's needs when they were young and now they are old enough to determine their own goals. We guided them in setting their goals in the same way we set individual, family, and marriage goals.

All of our goals needed to be in harmony with what was best for the family, and individual goals needed to exist in harmony with the goals of the other family members. It has taken a lot of talking, pondering, picturing, and clarifying to make this work. This has worked for us—and we know it has worked for other individuals, couples, and families.

The joy in creating a Goal Book is that it puts the tools in your hands so you can more effectively manage your life.

Creating a Goal Book is a simple task. A Goal Book is a visual record of the dreams and goals you have for yourself and/or your family. To create a Goal Book you simply need to:

- Ponder—define and visualize your goals and dreams
- Picture—find pictures to represent those goals
- Choose words that clarify your goals and dreams
- Glue the pictures and words on a sheet of paper
- Place the pages in a three-ring binder

At this point, your work of pondering and picturing is finished. You now sit back and wait for the forces of the universe to arrange your life, bringing you the goals that you envision, and thereby allowing you to prosper in life, love, and work.

Each page of your Goal Book can be a collage of pictures or a single picture that defines your goal. A Goal Book is a collection of everything you want in life wrapped up in one package. It is a reminder of why you are here and where you are going. It is a clear vision of the goals you intend to reach.

Reaching a goal is:

- One part defining what you want
- One part visualizing what you want that goal to look like when it is achieved
- One part preparing yourself to meet your goal
- One part miracle or magic

## If you make a Goal Book, will you get everything you ever wanted?

Not necessarily. A Goal Book is not a wish book. It is a book that contains words and pictures of the goals you want to achieve in life, love, and work. It isn't a place to put pictures of your endless shopping list.

## Is it okay to put extravagant things in your Goal Book?

Yes. Include all of your goals, even if they seem extravagant. My family and I wanted to travel around the world. We knew it was out of our price range and we couldn't imagine how we could afford it. We put this dream in our Goal Book and the universe worked out the details—the four of us traveled around the world in 2001.

## Can you include goals that you want immediately?

Yes, but the universe does not work on your (or my) timetable. It brings goals to you when you need them, not necessarily when you think you need them or want them. Just go with it.

Make your Goal Book pages and then sit back and relax. Someone else is driving.

### What if you mess up and include a goal that you later realize you don't want?

It will be all right. This is *your* Goal Book. If you put a goal in your book and then change your mind, you don't have to follow through with it when it comes to you. It isn't as though you wake up each day and get whisked from goal to goal. It will take time for each of your goals to come to you. While you are preparing and waiting for your goals to arrive, you will have the opportunity to focus on individual goals to determine if each goal is still what you really want. If you find that you no longer desire one of your goals, just remove that page from your Goal Book.

### What if you make pages incorrectly? Will bad things be brought to you?

It has been my experience that Goal Books bring good things, not bad. The intent of your goals should be to bring happiness and fulfillment into your life. When you construct your Goal Book pages, they should be filled with goals that are positive.

### Is goal setting like praying?

Goal setting is not like praying. Goal setting does not take the place of prayer. Prayer is something between you and God and you can pray for yourself or others. Goal setting is something you do for yourself in an effort to achieve your dreams and goals. It is a way for you to focus on what you want to accomplish in your life. (I am quite sure, however, that some higher power *does* have a hand in helping us achieve our goals.)

### If you put goals in your Goal Book will they just happen?

Creating pictures of your goals and placing them in your Goal Book is one step in the process of goal achievement. It defines what you want to achieve and then helps remind you where you are going. It helps you *catch* your goals by keeping you focused and reminding the universe of what is important to you. A Goal Book helps open doors of opportunity. When those doors are open, you must have the courage to walk through them and do the work necessary to achieve your goals.

## Why a Goal Book Works

The creation of a Goal Book is based on the belief that you know what is best for you. You are the only person who truly understands yourself and what you need. Don't be afraid to listen to yourself or to desire what you know you need and want.

Put your goals in your Goal Book and then sit back and wait as opportunities for achieving those goals come to you. Don't write step-by-step plans on how or when you will achieve a goal. I know, we are often taught to set a goal and to give ourselves benchmarks to chart our success. That is one method, using a Goal Book is another.

A Goal Book helps attract your goal. Once the opportunity for achieving your goal presents itself, then you must help by outlining the steps necessary to accomplish the goal, such as applying for admission to college, applying for scholarships, applying for a passport—items that would appear on a to-do list.

Trying to formulate a plan to attract and achieve your goals can be difficult because your problem-solving skills are limited by your experiences. Let the universe work out the details. The universe is infinite.

I use the phrase "Let the universe work out the details." You may have heard this concept expressed in one of the following ways:

"Put it in the hands of God."

"It will all work out in the end."

"Have faith."

"It will all come out in the wash."

You are free to apply whatever explanation you believe for why visualizing goals allows them to be achieved. You can find books that are filled with scientific information on brain patterns and theory based in science on why this works. You can find even more books based on religious doctrine, from various religions around the world, on why visualizing through prayer works. Whatever your beliefs, religious convictions, or scientific leanings, visualizing your goals helps them become real because there are forces greater than mere humans at work in the universe.

I don't know why it works. I think that when we set goals and visualize them, it connects us with that great conductor in the universe who orchestrates our lives, gently coaxing each note at the precise moment to create a beautiful symphony. I don't have a definitive answer. I just know I've witnessed its success in my life and the lives of others.

Nearly everyone believes that we can receive things we wish for. We've often been told "Be careful what you wish for, you just might get it." It is usually issued as a warning rather than given as a tool to be used constructively. Making a Goal Book offers the opportunity to carefully wish for the goals you really want—because you might get them.

The success of a Goal Book is a theory. It is not an exact science. It works for me. It works for my family. And, it has worked for friends and coworkers. It works for all of us.

In fact, I'd have to say that at least once a day I am part of a conversation about the success of a Goal Book. Someone asks about my successes or they share their success or discuss what page they are currently constructing. They tell me about a friend or a relative who made a Goal Book and the success they have had. Every day I hear about the joy that a Goal Book has brought to someone. People often ask me for guidance with creating their Goal Books. Well, here it is.

## Summary

- A Goal Book is composed of pictures and words that represent your vision of how you would like your life to unfold.
- A Goal Book is a tool to remind you where you are going in life.
- A Goal Book is a collection of everything you want in life wrapped up in one package.
- Don't include solutions for your goals in your Goal Book. Your problem-solving skills are limited by your experience.
- After you have constructed your Goal Book, let the universe work out the details.

# Two

# Let's Get Started

Goals are dreams with attitude. *Attitude* is the belief that your dreams will happen. *Attitude* is the courage to hope. *Attitude* is the determination to believe. *Attitude* is the difference between can't and can. *Attitude* is the difference between imagining and doing; between wishing and achieving. *Attitude* is the difference between a dream and a goal.

Setting goals and maintaining the attitude that they will happen are the first steps in determining where you want life to take you. If you are passionate about a dream and expect to reach your goals, you need to have enough attitude to walk the path, even if it is unclear.

The first thing you must do before constructing a Goal Book is to define your hopes, dreams, and goals. This requires thought. To help you with this task, we will look at the following areas:

- Where goals come from
- Reasons for setting goals
- Fear in goal setting
- How to construct a list of goals

## Where Do Goals Come From?

*Goals are your dreams, spun from your past.*

Goals come from listening to your self and paying attention to your dreams. Listening to your dreams allows you to reach within your self and discover what is best for you. It allows you to awaken the deep desires that will enable you to live a life you love. Listening to your dreams lets you determine your own path and find joy in walking that path. It gives you the liberty to make your own decisions and determine your destiny.

Dreaming dreams and setting them as your goals allows you to awaken your hidden splendor. That is what life is about.

Everyone has tremendous energy—sometimes it just needs to be awakened. All of us can find happiness and harmony—we just need to see the way. We need to listen to ourselves and pay attention to where we want to go with our goals.

It is your job to define what you want in life, and then you can let go of worrying about it and let the universe work out the details of bringing your goals to you. Life can be your masterpiece or it can be a collection of random actions that have come your way. Don't go through life as a pinball launched into the game and then propelled in whichever direction the greatest force thrusts you.

There are two ways to look at life:

"This is what I have—learn to live with it." or

"This is what I want—how can I get there?"

By setting goals, you take charge of your life and visualize where you want your life to take you. Life should be your masterpiece, so trust the universe to work out how you get to where you would like to be.

I believe I was born with goals; at some level I always knew they existed. When I review my childhood, there are certain memories that are clear, bright lines in my history. They are defining events that earned that designation because I innately knew they were leading me toward or away from my goals. I think I was actually at a crossroads at those defining moments and I remember them because they launched me on new paths.

Think back on your most significant memories. Consider if they were launch pads for moving you toward or away from where you knew you were going. You may never have consciously defined your goals, yet you probably knew whether those life events were consistent with your desires.

As you ponder your goals, remember:

- You are your own goal-setting boss. Be a worthy leader.
- Believe that you *can*, not that you *can't*.
- Remember, the best part of your life could be ahead of you.
- When you picture what you think is impossible, it just might become possible.

## Earliest Goals

When we are young, we don't see limits and problems. We see only possibilities. Think back on the possibilities that you saw when you were young. This will help you understand how to capture some of those dreams that you've put away because you thought they weren't possible.

My first goal was to buy a suitcase. I was in the third grade and imagined that I would travel the world. To me, the most essential item for traveling was a suitcase. I planned how I would accomplish this goal by first looking at how much a suitcase cost. I visualized my goal only to the extent that I focused my attention on a picture of the suitcase in a catalog. I saved my allowance, asked my parents and grandparents for money-earning jobs, and looked almost every day at the picture of the suitcase I intended to buy. After six months of saving, I bought my first suitcase, which served me well for many years.

At the age of nine, I didn't know that I was visualizing nor did I realize the powerful role visualization plays. Yet, there are many significant memories of me looking at the suitcase, counting the money I had saved, reading the description in the catalog, and finally, watching my mother write the order for the suitcase. It has only been in recent years that I have evaluated the significance of goal setting and visualizing in that experience.

## Next Goals: College and Europe

I had a dry spell in goal setting until I was in seventh grade. I thought about what I wanted in my life and wrote the goals of earning a Bachelor's degree and going to Europe. Actually, the trip to Europe was partially visualized through the use of a book that my mother had. It was a book with pictures of various locations around the world. In fact, it was the same book that inspired me to buy the suitcase in the third grade. I often studied the pictures and imagined myself in those locations. I was especially fond of visualizing myself in London and Paris. I even found maps of the two cities and studied them so I would know my way around—just in case I was ever lucky enough to go. I went so far as to practice speaking English with a French accent because, who knew, it could be useful when I went to Europe. Well, it made sense at the time!

Going to college seemed to be a goal that had a better chance of happening than the goal of going to Europe. My parents actually taught me to visualize attending college. They often spoke matter-of-factly about it. "When you're in college . . ." or "You'll learn that when you're in college." When I was about twelve, I remember asking my mother a question that required an answer based in physics. Her response was that she didn't know, and I would need to remember that question and ask it when I took science classes in college. My parents spoke of college with the same sense of confidence that they used when speaking about when I "grew up." They planted a vision of a goal that I adopted. I mentally visualized myself at college and at my college graduation ceremony; however, I never looked for pictures to place in a Goal Book. At that time, I didn't understand the importance of visualization.

During my high school and college years, I had clearly written goals. It was easier for me to make decisions about other opportunities when I had my eye on my goals. If an opportunity that presented itself didn't assist me in reaching one of these two goals—Bachelor's degree or a trip to Europe—then it was easy to say no.

I had a deep understanding that a Bachelor's degree was my first priority and everything else that was not consistent with this goal would have to wait. I had my goals written in a notebook and looked at them often to remind myself where I was going.

At the end of my junior year in college, the department in which I was majoring offered a travel-study course to Europe for a few weeks. This was the first time the department offered a trip of *any* kind. I couldn't believe that Europe was within my grasp. As you may have guessed, the trip included London and Paris and, because I had been preparing for this goal for years, I was prepared to walk around the cities without a map.

My parents were careful money managers and, at this point in time, going to Europe was regarded as an extravagant once-in-a-lifetime experience. I can clearly remember the night I discussed the idea with my mother. I knew my goal had been brought to me and that I was at a crossroads—with my parents' blessing being the pivotal factor.

I was home from college for the weekend and my mother and I were preparing dinner. I casually mentioned that I had an opportunity to go to Europe, along with an explanation of my portion of financial backing and how I would work extra jobs to help pay for the remaining amount. She listened and said that she would talk with my father later that night. The next morning she delivered the verdict. It was yes!

This was not only the realization of a huge goal, it also proved to be a pivotal time in my life that would forever alter the paths I would walk. It opened the door to a life filled with travel.

## Bigger and Better Goals

After achieving my two major goals, I gained confidence to expand my perception of what was possible. I was energized by my prosperity. Once I realized that setting goals enabled me to flourish and succeed, it empowered me to ponder more goals.

My next goals were exaggerations of the first two. I was relatively new at goal success, so I set goals that felt comfortable. My new goals were to get a Master's degree and to return to Europe to travel more extensively. These were a stretch for me because I was no longer living in my parents' home and was without their financial support.

I wrote both goals in a notebook. Within a short time, opportunities for both came to me, along with scholarships and other monetary support to pay for them. At this time, I was aware that having written goals was helpful, but I didn't realize the strategic significance of using pictures.

# The Vision of Your Future

A scrapbook preserves the precious memories from your past. A Goal Book ignites the excitement of your future. If you want more fond memories in your scrapbooks, then you have to put visions in your Goal Book. You must dare to dream and have the courage to liberate your dreams.

Oftentimes people oppress the dreams they find most exciting because they think there is no chance of them ever happening. Find those dreams and set them free on the pages of your Goal Book.

We are not taught to dream. We are usually taught to suppress our dreams with weighty tales by well-meaning family and friends of why our dreams will never come to fruition. They don't want us to be disappointed if we don't reach our goals. Instead, we are disappointed for never trying. We learn to put our dreams away and quietly accept the life of a pinball.

All you have in life is this moment. As you move from moment to moment, it is a gentle weaving of threads from your past into hopes for your future. Look at your history, what you have, what you've accomplished, what you've learned, and use that information to create the vision of your future. By recognizing the vision of your future, you can adjust your actions to assist yourself in moving into that hope-filled future.

When you consider your life history, recall fond memories of significant events. These events were probably when you felt a sense of accomplishment. They were when you met your goals. Visualize how you felt when your goal was achieved. These are the conditions that you want to capture when creating pages for your Goal Book.

Remember the wonderful excitement of the moment, the happiness and the joy. These are the elements that should be present when you ignite the dreams of your future. Recall the circumstances that created a happy past, envision that mood in your future, and weave it into your life today.

Take a few hours to determine what is important to you and what you want in life. After doing this, you can then construct your Goal Book pages. You've probably spent more time deciding on a new pair of shoes—so, no excuses! If you don't take the time to ponder, the universe probably won't take much time to send things your way.

When you're quiet and alone you can hear the whispers of your soul. It may be when you first awaken in the morning, or when you're basking in the sunlight, or driving your car. When you hear the same messages over and over, these are your goals. Pay attention. They are calling to you.

Listen. Can you hear them? Can you hear your hopes and dreams speaking softly, hoping you'll let them live? Don't keep them locked up any longer. Let them come out and delight you with their presence. Dreams are not meant to be locked away.

I have had the goal of publishing parenting books for thirty years. It calls to me when I'm alone. It speaks to me when I'm working in the garden or when I'm cooking dinner. I think about mysteries of life that I know I'm destined to research and discover.

I have listened for thirty years. I have also talked myself out of writing for thirty years. There is always a reason. I felt I couldn't write as an authority without a PhD, my children were young and needed me to be with them (these were conflicting goals and my *core* goal was caring for my children), I couldn't quit a well-paying job to write, I didn't feel I had enough time to write and work full-time. There were many *excuses* I used as *reasons*.

Yet, it was always there. When I was alone, I heard the call. I thought I would get over it and find contentment in other things. I didn't get over it. Finally, my children were grown. I had spent appropriate time parenting them and preparing them to be fine adults who could be sent into the future. My only excuse was the need to maintain a well-paying job because it seemed foolish to give up a job to write and promote books when I was so near retirement. And then it happened in the most unexpected of ways. My job ended. I was given the gift of time. The universe had arranged the details. I was free to write. The voices quieted. I was finally on the path that had been calling me for thirty years.

Listen to your voices. Heed their call. They won't go away. You have a purpose. You must get on with it.

Being too busy is the enemy of your goals and your creativity because the noise from moving too fast blocks the quiet voices that guide you. When you're moving too fast you develop "scatter disorder." That's when you feel scattered and just can't get a handle on anything. You feel out of control. Sometimes you cry or become angry and aggressive because you can't get a grip on your life.

Slow down. Patiently listen to yourself. You know what's best for you. You are a child of the universe and the universe speaks to you. Make time to listen. Accept what you hear.

## NO, NO, NO!

As soon as infants and toddlers begin to move, adults tell them, "No!" Children are told what not to touch, where they can't go—everything is off-limits. As children grow older and begin to express their own opinions, they are often told their opinions aren't valid. A teenager might say he is hungry and a parent will say, "You can't be hungry, we just ate." Another might express that she is cold and an adult will tell her that she can't be cold because it's eighty degrees outside.

We are told not to be angry, not to be upset, not to feel sad, and not to feel many of the emotions we feel. The list goes on and on and we are conditioned not to trust our feelings and ourselves. That's how we learn not to trust our dreams. We decide they must not be valid either.

I am encouraging you to let go of all that learning—and trust your self. Trust that you know what is best for you and create a lovely Goal Book that celebrates what you want your life to be.

- Allow yourself to dream.
- Allow those around you to dream their own dreams.
- Listen to your dreams.
- Set your dreams as goals and expect them to happen.
- Have attitude and believe.

## Reasons for Setting Goals

If you want some influence over your life, then you must set goals. It might be easier to just get up each day and see where that day leads you rather than meet each day with a purpose. Sometimes, it is even exciting to live life not knowing where the path will lead. However, most people find little satisfaction in living their lives without guidance because they experience few rewards.

Feelings of reward often come when you have an accomplishment. Accomplishments are more complex than completing tasks. For example, you may feel a sense of accomplishment when you finish the laundry and all of the clothes are clean. I've found that this is a short-lived reward, though, because a new "rewarding" laundry day looms on the horizon as soon as anyone in the family changes his or her clothes. Daily tasks are rarely the rewards we seek.

Goals are composed of things greater than tasks on a daily to-do list. You set goals because a month from now or a year from now you want your life to be a little more reflective of the perfection you imagine.

You have a vision of a perfect life. Setting goals encourages you to get up each morning with a vision of that perfection so you can remember where you are headed. This vision guides you toward a greater accomplishment, even while you are doing the tasks of daily living.

When you identify a goal and begin to speak about it, this somehow activates forces that help make it happen. It connects an energy that flows among many people to help your goal come to you.

When our children were ages seven and nine we wanted them to learn a language other than English, even though foreign languages were not offered at their elementary school. We decided on French. We had friends over for dinner and the topic of foreign language came up. We discussed our goal with them. Our friends managed a summer youth camp and about two months later they called and said they had the name of a girl from Belgium who had applied for a job with them. They didn't have a position available for her, but her cousins had attended the camp and our friends felt she would be a reliable person. They talked to the cousins and were told that she wanted to spend time in the United States to practice her English.

We contacted this young woman and extended an invitation for her to stay with our family for a few weeks in the summer so she could work on her English and our children could practice French. A beautiful friendship was born. It is one that we have maintained since 1991. I believe it came about because we set a goal, visualized the goal, expected it to happen, and then let the universe work out the details.

## What Exactly Is a Goal?

Goals are conditions that you want or need, or things for which you have a passion. We all want our basic needs to be met. Beyond our basic needs, we have wants. We need housing of some sort. We *want* a bigger house or more than one house. We need food.

We *want* to go to fine restaurants. We need clothing. We *want* designer fashions. I think you get the idea.

Basic needs are those things we must have for survival, and then we set goals for the things we want that will make our lives more comfortable—or even extravagant.

Passions are more difficult to define. Passions are what you think about whenever you have the opportunity. Everyone has a passion for something. Fortunately, passions are different, so we aren't all pursuing the same goal. Even if you must overcome misfortunes, you can still pursue your passions. When you have a passion for something, you don't have to be told to do it. You are naturally attracted to your passions. You find yourself thinking about your passions when you're doing things that are less attractive.

Your passions are your goals. Your goals are what you think about when you daydream.

When you think back on your life, you have always known what was best for you. Memories are strongest when they are filled with emotion. Those strong memories probably represent when you knew you were moving toward or away from a goal. Take a few minutes and think about some of the memories during various stages in your life. Write them down. I'm sure you'll see a pattern. You'll find memories that you define as *happy* and memories that you define as *sad* or *bad*. Those happy memories moved you toward the life you knew you wanted and those sad or bad memories moved you away from where you wanted your life to be. You have always known what was best for you.

Without knowing it or thinking about it, at some level you have defined a direction for your life. Your goals are those events and conditions that move you in the directions you *feel* and may have always felt are right for you. A goal is like a beacon of light. It is in the distance and guides you. Each day you can measure whether you are moving toward or away from that beacon of light. Your goals are always with you. Your goals always guide you.

# Fear in Goal Setting

We often fear setting goals. We fear facing our true hopes and dreams and actually admitting to ourselves that those are the things we want most in life. We fear the disapproval of others who may think what we want is foolish or unrealistic. Mostly, though, we fear failure.

When we admit what we want, we may have to acknowledge that we are not where we would like to be in life. We may have to face the fact that we have not been loyal to our own goals. We may have to admit to ourselves that we've been pinballs.

What if you admit to yourself the goals you desire most and put them in a Goal Book and they don't happen? Then you have to admit failure. But, even if you don't put your goals in a Goal Book and they don't happen, you still fail. At least if they are in your Goal Book and you pay attention to them every day, there is a much better chance that they will happen.

You may put desired accomplishments in your book that involve a commitment on your part. Maybe something like getting a Master's degree. If you put that in as a goal and the universe brings you the opportunity to attain the degree, you would actually have to do the work to earn the degree.

Sometimes people fear if they awaken the enormity of their true desires they may not have the strength to keep up with the realization. Don't be afraid. When you are doing what you love and desire, an inner strength is unleashed in proportion to the energy necessary to achieve your goal. You will have the strength to dance into the night enjoying your dreams and goals as they are realized. You will find energy in the excitement of inventing what is you.

Sometimes we set goals only half-believing that they will actually come to us. When you include a goal in your Goal Book, you must be prepared to fulfill your part of the goal responsibility when it comes to you. Drifting is not an option. Achieving goals is not a place for a passive spectator. It requires a belief and attitude that your goals will be accomplished. For example, let's say you put a trip to Paris in your Goal Book. You can talk yourself out of such a trip with fears about language barriers, jet lag, or not knowing the city. It may seem much easier to stay home. When you are passionate and really want a goal, a little jet lag won't be a problem.

Sometimes people are afraid to choose goals because they fear making the wrong choice. What if you do make a choice that you later discover you don't like? Unless it is a huge life-altering goal, you can always change your mind and set a new goal.

The only permanent life-altering goal I can imagine is the birth of a child. Everything else can be changed. It may not be easy to reconcile past decisions, but they can be changed. It's not as though you are stuck with the same goals forever without change. If a goal comes to you and you can't do it at that time, or you have changed your mind—don't do it. Life changes every day.

Remember, these are *your* goals. You can change them, adjust them, or disregard them whenever you want. These goals are *yours*.

Many people fear setting goals because they are afraid of what family and friends will think if they actually do what they long to do. I had a chemistry professor who sang to us during lab classes. He had a wonderful voice and probably should have been singing professionally. I asked him about it one day and he told me his father worked in a science-related field and very much wanted him to have a career in science also. He wanted to sing, but didn't want to disappoint his father, so instead, he disappointed himself and every day he longed for reaching his own goal. He was a pinball and went in the direction the greatest force pushed him, that force being his father.

Ponder what you want, write it down, picture it, make a goal page, and walk bravely as the universe brings you the opportunity to achieve your goal. Define your own success. Declare your own victories. Enjoy your prosperity.

## Great Expectations

The first part of goal setting is creating your list of goals. If you are in a relationship, both people need to work on the list together because you are working for the good of the relationship, not necessarily for the good of the individual in isolation (See Chapter 6). If you are in a family with children over the age of seven, set your goals as a couple first, and then set your goals as a family. Your life is complex and intertwines with the lives of many other people. You can't set goals for one area of your life without considering the impact on those to whom you are closely attached.

When personal goals are achieved, they can affect your family members, friends, and coworkers. Everyone who will be involved when the goals are achieved should be considered when the goals are set.

To get started on your list, relax, sit quietly, and listen to yourself. Don't be afraid of what you hear. When you look into your soul and accept what you see, it is a powerful tool for goal setting. Don't be afraid to accept what you see and desire. When you evaluate what you have accomplished in your life and hear yourself saying things like, "I wish I would have (done something)," or "I wish I could (do something)"; whatever follows these phrases is probably a goal.

I suggest that you begin your list by taking a couple of days to ponder the core goals in your life (See Chapter 3). It may be hard to find reflective time since, like most of people today, you are probably overscheduled and moving as fast as you can to keep up. Make time to define your core list and create a few pages that reflect those goals. You can then continue to schedule time to add more pages and determine new items to add to your list.

Putting your goals in a Goal Book is simply effective communication with the universe. Without written and visualized goals, it is a little like asking a person to hand you that "thing." When there are so many things to choose from, they wouldn't know which one to give you.

The same is true with the universe. There are so many things to choose from that the universe couldn't possibly know which one you want unless you identify it. The universe is like an air traffic controller. You actually have to ask to land and take off. Simply circling the airport or taxiing the runway will not make landing and taking off happen. You have to specifically make your request known to the person in charge.

When you write down your goals they are illusive visions within your mind. When you read them, the mental images can change depending on your mood. The unique aspect of placing your goals into a Goal Book is that for the first time you have taken an image that only you see in your mind and turned it into something real that exists in this world.

You can look at your goal, experience it, and share that vision with others. Placing pictures of the vision of your goal into your Goal Book is the transitional step that allows you to actually see your goal in this world. For most of us, seeing is believing. This step allows your dreams to come alive.

## As you set out to achieve your goals

- Enlist some cheerleaders to encourage you when you forget where you are going.
- Don't listen to those who boo you for trying. (Sometimes there are more people who boo than cheer.)
- Believe in your goals and patiently await their arrival.
- Know it is easier to make choices about opportunities when you have your goals in place because they serve as filters.

- Remember your goals every day so you can follow the path the universe has brought you.
- Understand that when your goals are in place, you can see how events fit into their achievement. Crossroads appear when your goals are brought to you. You choose whether or not to accept them.
- Revisit your goals often to remind yourself what is important to you. Goals serve as a guide and renew your strength when the going gets tough.

## I'm Not Sure What I Want

I have often observed that it is difficult for people to define what they want—although most of us know all too clearly what we *don't* want. If you aren't sure what you want, it is helpful to ask yourself, "If I could have only one thing in my life the way I want it, what would it be?" The answer to this question will require some pondering. After you determine your most important goal, then do the same thing to add a second and a third and as many as you like.

You might be surprised what this list reveals. Note: If your first goal is to buy a sports car, think some more. Is this really the most important goal in your life—if you could have only one goal? You may choose differently if one goal is all you can attain.

Usually people come up with basic goals such as good health, happiness, love, longevity, and enough money to pay their bills. These are what I call core goals. These goals are the ones you must have because without them all the materialism in the world won't matter because you couldn't enjoy it.

Sometimes when people are trying to set their goals, I hear them say that they want more money, or more time, or more energy. The real question is, what would you do if you had more money, time, or energy? By answering these questions you are creating your list of goals. Having more money, time, and energy are useless—unless you spend them on those things that you desire.

Many people say they want to win the lottery. A mountain of money isn't what they really want. They want money to give them freedom from the daily grind of working so they can do the things they enjoy. They also want to have enough money so they don't have to struggle for the necessities and can enjoy some of the luxuries they desire.

Creating a Goal Book allows you to determine how you want to spend that money. Sometimes unexpected money comes to you. When you have your goals in order, unexpected money isn't really unexpected. You already know how it will be spent because you have identified your goals. You are simply awaiting its arrival.

Goals also help you identify the things you want that money can't buy. Even with a mountain of money, you won't have fulfilling relationships, good health, longevity, and a peaceful life. It is very important to think about your entire life when you are generating your list. Be sure to consider all of the aspects of your life that require a goal. Your list needs to include your personal relationships, your job, your hopes, and your dreams.

## Tasks versus Goals

It is easy to confuse daily deadlines and the demands of life with goals. We often have a full to-do list. At the end of the day or week, we can look and see all of the items checked off and feel like we've achieved our goals. We can accomplish many *tasks* yet never achieve our *goals*. It is easy to confuse being over-scheduled and stressed with accomplishment. Many of our tasks can involve several steps, yet still only be tasks on a to-do list.

However, in some cases, tasks may be part of a goal. Take holiday cards, for example. Sending holiday cards involves buying the cards and stamps, addressing them, signing them and/or writing notes in them, and then mailing them. This can take several days. Accomplishing this task may simply be the completion of an item on your to-do list and not part of a goal—however, if staying in touch with friends or brightening someone's life is a goal for you, then the activity of sending holiday cards has contributed to maintaining that goal.

Examine your to-do lists and compare them to your goals. If you are spending lots of time doing things that aren't part of your goals, you have either identified the wrong goals or you are wasting precious time walking on a path that isn't leading toward your goals.

To generate your goal list, ask yourself (remember, if you are in a partnership or family, you need to do this together):

- If I could have only one thing in my life the way I want it, what would it be?
- If I could have a second thing in my life the way I want it, what would it be?
- Add as many desires as you can think of.
- If I had more money, what would I do with it?
- If I had more time, what would I do with it?
- If I had more energy, what would I do?
- What kind of work do I enjoy?
- What does the perfect job look like?
- What kind of person/people do I want to spend my life with?
- In what kind of home/environment do I want to live?
- What does happiness look like to me?
- Where would I like to travel?
- What accomplishments do I want to achieve?

Write down everything you want in life. I mean everything. This could be a long list that seems unmanageable. Now, sort the list. Some things you wrote aren't goals; they belong on a to-do list.

Your list might look something like this:

*Clean the garage*

*Get a new job*

*Lose weight*

*Buy groceries*

*Do the laundry*

*Buy a new car*

*Be happy*

*Travel to Mexico*

*Mow the lawn*

*Have a good marriage*

*Remodel the kitchen*

*Get a Bachelor's degree*

*Replace a button on my blue suit*

*Plant bulbs in the garden*

*Read a book*

*Travel to Europe*

Some of these items are goals and take time to achieve, while others can go on a to-do list:

*Buy groceries*

*Do laundry*

*Mow the lawn*

*Replace a button on my blue suit*

"Plant bulbs" probably belongs on a to-do list. However, if you really meant, "create a garden," then it belongs in your Goal Book. Depending on the condition of your garage, "clean the garage" may belong on the to-do list. However, I have seen many garages that required a page in the Goal Book because they needed to be completely reorganized and it was going to take a lot of motivation and more than a couple of hours of work. "Read a book" belongs on a to-do list; unless the intent of that item was to establish a pattern of reading regularly, then it belongs in your Goal Book.

All of the other items on the list need to have a page in your Goal Book. You will need to visualize how you want each of these items to look when they are completed. Simply listing what you want without visualizing how you want each item to look when it is achieved is an incomplete way to set goals. Visualization is essential in defining what you want in life.

I know a woman who wanted to be married. She talked to her friends and told them she would really like to find a man to marry. They kept introducing her to men of various ages, types, and sizes. She was not interested in any of them. She finally realized that she wasn't interested in just *any* man, she had one in mind who possessed particular qualities. She was able to visualize the qualities of the relationship she hoped to find, which helped define the qualities of the person she would be interested in meeting. Now, she's getting somewhere.

## Summary

- Goals come from listening to yourself and paying attention to your dreams.
- Pondering your dreams and setting them as your goals allows you to awaken your hidden splendor.
- Making a Goal Book ignites excitement for your future.
- By recognizing the vision of your future, you can adjust your actions to assist yourself in moving into a hope-filled future.
- Set your own goals. Don't disappoint yourself.
- People are conditioned to not trust their feelings and dreams.
- You will find little satisfaction living without goals because you will experience few rewards.
- Speaking about your goals somehow activates the forces that make them happen.
- Goals are conditions that you want or need, or things for which you have a passion.
- Your goals are those things that you think about when you daydream.
- Goal setting doesn't allow drifting through life.
- We fear setting goals because we fear what family and friends will think of our goals.
- Look deep into your soul and accept what you see. Those are your goals.
- You are speaking about your goals when you say, "I wish I could . . .," or "I wish I would have . . ."

- Setting goals is simply effective communication with the universe.
- Placing pictures of your goals into a Goal Book allows them to come alive.
- Most of us know what we *don't* want. Setting goals helps you define what you *do* want.
- Many people say they want more money; the important question is how would they spend the money if they had it.
- People often confuse deadlines and life's demands with goals.
- It is your job to define what you want in life; it is the job of the universe to work out the details.

So, ponder your dreams, get some attitude, picture your goals, and get started!

# THREE

# Defining Goals

When we set goals, we often list events such as graduation, marriage, the birth or adoption of a child, a new job, a trip, a promotion, or retirement from a job. We spend a lot of time planning and imagining these events. Events are certainly goals. But then they become triggers for the years of *continuation* or state-of-being goals that follow. People can spend months, even years in some cases, planning these life events; however, few spend time pondering how the years to follow one of these events will look.

I knew a young woman in her late twenties who felt her biological clock ticking. It told her that she needed to soon marry and have children if she were intending to do so. She created a Goal Book and included pages representing a wedding, a new car, a new house, and a baby. In just a few months, she met a very nice man and they married. A few months after their marriage, they bought a new car and by the next year they had a baby and a new house. The unfortunate part is they didn't visualize their lives beyond these events and didn't create Goal Book pages for their life together.

They both focused on the wedding and visualized the beautiful day they would share with family and friends. They visualized the birth of their baby and the wonderful event it would be. They visualized the house and the new car. They did not, however, share visions of their marriage or their roles as parents. They didn't visualize the realities of ongoing maintenance and repair of a house. They didn't visualize the daily routine of their lives.

At this time, I'm sad to say, they have a frustrating marriage that appears to bring neither of them the satisfaction they desire. Although the life events of marriage, birth, new house, and new car were exactly as they had pictured, they neglected to imagine the most important part: the years of life that followed the events of their lives.

## TYPES OF GOALS

There are three categories of goals and each requires its own set of pages in your Goal Book. They are *core, event,* and *continuation* goals.

### Core Goals

The first and most important goals are *core goals*. These are goals that are conditions in our lives, such as good health, happiness, love, harmony, prosperity, safety, tranquility, and longevity. They are the veils that we hope will grace each day of our lives.

Core goals are essential to our existence. They are the goals that without which life would have little meaning and bring little joy. They create the tone for each day we exist. They are the goals that we desire from the moment of our birth. They need to be a part of each page in your Goal Book. They need to be present in each event goal to set the mood for the event. They need to be present in your continuation goals to provide meaning to your existence.

You must define your core goals and create a picture of how they will look when they exist. You can't hold happiness in your hands, so it is hard to describe. And, the definition of happiness changes depending on who is describing it. You must imagine how your life looks when you are happy. Imagine life at home and life at work. Visualize what makes you happy and then create Goal Book pages defined by your vision of happiness.

It is important to imagine how all of your core goals look to you. I have a friend who created a Goal Book page for a beautiful garden. She wanted more than just a flower garden; she wanted a beautiful serenity garden. She had an image in her mind of how serenity would look in her yard. She created her Goal Book page for a garden and veiled it with serenity. The components she needed for her garden began to come to her. She received several trees from a friend, so she could create a backdrop for her vision of serenity. She had paving stones in front of the house. In her vision, they didn't belong there, so she moved them to the backyard. She had bushes on the side of her house that didn't belong there in her vision, so she moved them, too. She rearranged her assets in such a way that her vision of a beautiful serenity garden was realized.

Note: Her vision of a garden may be different from the vision that you have for a garden. That is why it is important to picture your desires and define them through your core goals.

## Event Goals

The next category is an *event goal*. These are goals that are usually the result of hard work and planning or a one-time happening in your life. Event goals include such things as graduation, a new job, a job promotion or job change, marriage, birth or adoption of a child, a trip, buying a house or a car, being accepted into a college program, or retiring from a job.

We usually measure the success of our lives by the achievement of event goals. We look at these as the milestones of our success. We remember them because they are the punctuation in our days of sameness. Life is a series of routines, little of which we remember. Events are the stuff of which most memories are made.

Think of events as lane shifts. Imagine that you are driving a car. An event would move you into a different traffic lane or it may merge you onto a new road altogether.

Event goals reshape your future either on a short- or long-term basis. Events, such as trips, usually have a short-term effect on your life. You shift lanes for a week or two and then you're back on the same road you were traveling before the vacation. Other events, such as graduation from high school or college, a new job, marriage, divorce, birth or adoption of a child, or retirement from a job can launch you onto entirely new roads.

People have relatively few events in their lives, yet events produce most of the changes we experience. We mark our time on earth with events. We count the numbers of birthdays and wedding anniversaries. We count the number of years at a job. We count our children. We count the numbers of marriages and divorces. We define our existence by the events we experience. We document our lives through photos tracking these events.

It is essential that you think through your event goals to ensure they define who you really want to be.

So that you can understand the power of a Goal Book, I will tell you about some travel successes that came to us after we visualized them and placed them in our Goal Book.

My family created pages in our Goal Book of places we wanted to go and then the universe worked out the details of getting us there.

We love to travel and always have four or five trips planned because we never know which one the universe will bring to us. It doesn't pay to be unprepared, because we could miss a great opportunity. We go to a discount bookstore and buy outdated travel books at a reduced cost for planning purposes. The winters are really long in Northern Michigan, so we spend those dreary months planning our trips. We use travel brochures and pictures from magazines to create pages of the places we want to visit. We also have tentative itineraries ready so we can refine them when we actually learn the location the universe has brought us. We then sit back and wait to see which destination goes on sale at some ridiculous price or which airline offers a new route with promotional prices, or which friend moves to one of our goal destinations and invites us to visit.

We have often had several destinations brought to us in the same trip. In 1998, a friend took a job in Japan and half-jokingly told us to visit her if we had the chance. She really didn't know the forces she was enticing. She moved to Japan in January. In March, I was reading a travel magazine when I saw an ad for an attractively priced offer to visit Thailand. I called about it and for $50 we could add a stopover in Japan. I then received a mailing from an airline where we have frequent flyer miles. For 20,000 miles we could travel from Japan to Australia. We made calls, e-mailed our friend, phoned the airline, and finally put together a very cost-effective trip that included a visit to Thailand with a stopover in Japan (where we stayed with our friend). During the stopover, we flew with frequent flyer miles to Australia and back to Japan, and then used our original tickets to return home. This was all in our price range because so much of it was free, on sale, or off-season priced.

Before establishing a Goal Book, we never imagined that we could take our children on such a trip. Nor would we have intentionally tried to put together such an unlikely group of destinations and circumstances that resulted in making the trip possible for us. We could never have imagined those circumstances. It took the universe to orchestrate what turned out to be a spellbinding trip for our family.

We've found that just because we have only one page for a destination, it doesn't mean we'll accomplish the entire experience on a single trip. When we went to Thailand, we had to make choices about what to see and do because we had a limited amount of time. We were forced to miss a beautiful temple that was pictured in our Goal Book. After returning home, we saw many references to that temple and were disappointed that we had been in Bangkok and missed seeing it. To correct this error, two years later the universe arranged for a stopover in Bangkok with enough time for us to visit the missed temple!

On our first trip to China, the universe gave us a handsomely priced package tour. A year or two earlier, we had constructed a Goal Book page for China, with many historic landmarks that we wanted to visit. The tour we happened to get took us to the exact locations that were so beautifully displayed in our Goal Book.

We also had a Goal Book page for Hawaii. We constructed it a few years before we actually went. We took travel brochures and cut out pictures that we liked and constructed a page. We didn't know which islands the pictures were from or which islands we wanted to visit. When the universe took us to Hawaii, we went on a driving tour and pulled off where a sign indicated a waterfall. When we saw it, our kids were the first to recognize that it was the waterfall in our Goal Book. We were taken to the exact location without even knowing where it was!

## Continuation Goals

The third type is a *continuation goal.* Continuation goals are conditions in our lives that are usually triggered by an event. They are the routines of life that we don't remember specifically, yet they are the substance of our existence. They are the 365 breakfasts, lunches, and dinners we eat each year. They are the time we spend doing the hundreds of loads of laundry we wash in a year. They are the time spent in endless trips in the car, or sorting mail. They are the moments spent brushing our teeth, taking showers, and washing dishes. They are the hours we spend sitting in meetings, answering the phone, creating reports, and responding to emails.

Continuation goals lack the glamour of event goals and the grace of core goals. As a result, they are often overlooked in goal setting and planning, which can be disastrous. **Continuation goals need the most attention in your Goal Book because they are your life!**

Daily living often requires finding harmony between extremes. You either have nothing interesting to do, life is an endless routine; or you have too much to do and you are overwhelmed by chaos. You must find the essence that describes your continuation goals because continuation goals provide meaning and happiness to daily living—they sustain you.

Continuation goals are so difficult to capture in visualizations that it is a challenge for most people to create pages for them. This is probably because we remember our lives in *moments*. We don't remember whole days, weeks, or months. We remember certain moments within those days and months. Continuation goals require that you focus specifically on the mood you want for those days and months that represent the bulk of your life. Continuation goals require that you create the sequel for the event goal draped with your core goals—and you must do this with the same enthusiasm and planning that you used when preparing for the event that triggered this continuation.

I will use the example of a wedding, since weddings are some of the most visualized events throughout the world. If you ask people how they imagine their wedding to be, most can give you a detailed answer. Some people hire wedding planners to ensure their vision of the event occurs.

With no planning whatsoever, most people surmise that their marriage will be a continuation of the perfect wedding day. People falsely believe there is a direct relationship between the amount of time spent planning the wedding and the quality of the marriage. There is NO correlation. There is, however, a relationship between the amount of time spent planning the sequel to the wedding—that being the marriage and the success of the marriage. Visualize how "happily ever after" looks to you and your partner. Spend hours defining that look, and then create your Goal Book pages.

## Creating a Life You Will Love

When creating your Goal Book pages, wrap each event and continuation goal with your core goals. Illustrate your pages with your vision of perfection. Include happy faces that create the tone and mood you want in your daily life as well as in the events of your life. Spend as much time envisioning your daily life as you spend envisioning your events and I am sure you will find your days are much happier.

With visualization and planning, your goals can work throughout your life. Each one of us has a different idea of perfection. If you are sharing a continuation goal with a partner or other family members, you will need to spend time discussing what that condition looks like before you make the Goal Book page. Again, using the example of a wedding, we get lots of help imagining what the flowers will look like, the photos, the reception, and all the other aspects of the event. That's because we buy these services and the people selling them want to make us happy, so they help us picture what it will look like. They don't want us to arrive at our wedding day and find that the reality of what we bought doesn't meet the expectations of what we envisioned.

Unfortunately, you can't buy a happy marriage, and many couples arrive at their marriage only to find that it is nothing like their vision of what it would be like. You are on your own to create a satisfying life that meets your expectations. With that in mind, create the mood you want for your life and put it in your Goal Book. When you settle for less than your goals, it makes your whole life feel like second best.

As you define your event goals, you will need to expand them or create a corresponding page if there is a continuation goal that follows that event.

## The Best Things in Life Are Free

I've talked with many people about their goals and what they want in their lives. At first they think everything they want costs money and the only barrier to achieving their goals is a lack of money. Sometimes people confuse goals with materialism. People tell me that they really don't want the biggest house or the most expensive car. What they really want is a quiet, peaceful life filled with happiness and enough money so they can do the things they enjoy, without worrying about paying their bills and having enough money for retirement.

After making their lists, most of them discover that much of what they want doesn't require money. Their greatest desires have to do with happiness, love, health, confidence, competence, achievement, respect, and feeling good about themselves.

*The human soul craves what cannot be seen and can only be satisfied when those needs are met.*

How many times have you heard about a rich person who had every material possession, yet was miserable? We see this in the headlines almost every day.

*It is important to set goals for those things you cannot see.*

You may be confused because you are bombarded with messages

telling you that you should want bigger, better, and more. These messages can camouflage your true goals and cause you to feel uncertainty about whether your goals are valid. Your goals are *yours* and they are valid if they are valid to you.

On my first trip to China, I visited the hutongs in Beijing. What struck me most was the lack of materialism. There were community toilets and showers that were shared by the residents. People had to walk down the block to use them. I strolled amongst their homes and was even allowed to look inside a few. The door was open on one home and I could see inside. The house appeared to consist of one small room with a large closet in the corner. Outside the door, there was a little cooking grill that served as the kitchen, some jugs for carrying water, and caged chickens eating maggots on rotting tomatoes. The scene was one that I quickly categorized as extreme poverty and I imagined that the residents must be in a state of depression and hopelessness. As I came closer, I was invited to step inside to meet the occupants. There I saw a mother, father, and young child playing a board game on a bed that occupied eighty percent of the room. They were smiling and sharing a beautiful and serene family experience. They did not have the look of despair that I expected. They had a look of peace and happiness that I have seldom seen in the United States. They seemed happy!

That experience was a turning point in my life. I realized that happiness and success are not defined by materialism. Life is most rewarding when we define success by the quality of our relationships and whether we have a meaningful life filled with joy and happiness. As I listen closely to people in the United States, this is what many of us crave most.

## Visualizing

When you visualize your goal, imagine how you want it to look when it is achieved. You do this when you plan parties or activities of any kind. You visualize a picture of who will be there, happy faces, and a relaxed mood for the gathering. You visualize the goal as it will look when it is accomplished. Put that picture in your Goal Book. The faces and the mood you imagine. A goal looks at where you want to end up, which helps you determine where you must begin. Imagine how you will look and feel when you have accomplished your goal. Imagine your feelings of accomplishment and joy. Recapture those feelings each time you look at your goal page and hold onto those emotions until your goal is accomplished.

Another part of visualizing goals is that you heighten your awareness of what you are looking for so you recognize it when you see it. My son was interested in having a toy produced. He showed it to us and we had no idea how to go about producing toys. I told him to put it in his Goal Book and reminded him that determining what we want is our responsibility; working out the details is up to the universe. About a week later, a salesperson visited my office. During the course of our conversation, it was revealed that she developed toys that were used in her sales. My interest was piqued because I knew of my son's desire to have a toy produced, so I asked her how she went about it. She gave me the name of a contact person so we could begin the process. If I had not been aware of my son's desire, I wouldn't have recognized that she had information that would be useful in achieving his goal—or maybe, the universe would never have delivered her to my office.

My sister had a rewarding experience with visualization. Her in-laws had passed away and she and my brother-in-law prepared his parents' house for sale. The house was over a thousand miles away, so it was difficult to monitor. They listed the house with a real estate agent and were waiting for it to sell. My sister decided to visualize the sale of the house and made a page of that vision for her Goal Book. She glued a "sold" sign on a picture representing the house and placed the page in her Goal Book. The very next day the real estate agent phoned. The house had sold for their asking price!

## Summary

- There are three kinds of goals: Core goals, event goals, and continuation goals.
- Core goals are conditions in your life, such as good health, happiness, love, peace, harmony, prosperity, safety, tranquility, and longevity.
- Event goals are experiences that often reshape your life, like graduation and marriage.
- Continuation goals are conditions in your life that are usually triggered by an event, such as job satisfaction and getting along with your spouse.
- Continuation goals need the most attention in your Goal Book because they are your life.
- Define how each of your goals looks to you. (Everyone has a different definition.)
- You are responsible for creating a satisfying life that meets your expectations.
- When you settle for less than your goals, it makes your whole life feel like second best.
- Happiness and success don't have to be defined by materialism.

# FOUR

# Rules for Setting Goals

I have learned through personal experience that it is best to create pictures of what you want rather than to use only words. By illustrating a goal through the use of pictures, you can more accurately express how the achievement of the goal will look. If you use only words to describe your goal, you might leave out some very important points—and get the literal translation.

Let me explain. I was very busy at work and had many demands on my time. I worked a lot of extra hours and was exhausted. One of the goals on my list was to get more rest and not have to work so much. I included no pictures. What I received was the literal translation. I came down with an unusual virus and had no energy, which resulted in my having to miss a great deal of work and rest a lot! Although, what I really wanted was to be healthy and have my work schedule slow down. A picture could have shown that balance.

Another written goal I had was to spend more time with my children. The translation I received was that my husband had to live away from home for a few months and I virtually became a single parent. I spent more time with my children—through demands for transportation and basic care rather than sharing pleasant moments. My intent when I wrote the goal was that my husband and two children and I would share more time together talking, playing, and enjoying each other's company. I wanted to work less at my job so that I could be home more.

In each of these situations, visualized goals through the use of pictures would have more effectively illustrated on paper what I had in my mind. I have since found that using pictures more accurately conveys the mood and conditions that are part of my goals. I haven't had any misinterpretations since I started to use pictures that represent the visualization of my goals—although there have been some bonuses.

Let me give you three other examples. Let's say you write on a goal list that you want a new job. Well, that's probably what you will get—a new job as the result of being fired, downsized, or laid-off. Or, maybe the new job is worse than the one you had—when what you really wanted was to find a more rewarding job where you felt satisfaction and/or appreciation for your efforts.

Or, let's say you write down "I'd like to sleep late in the morning." Maybe what you meant is that you would like to sleep until you felt like getting up or that you would prefer not to have to get up at 6:00 a.m. to go to work every day. But, without a visual clarification, you might end up getting a night job and still be sleep deprived.

Finally, maybe you write "I'd like to lose ten pounds." Be sure to use a picture or you could get a literal translation and end up having surgery to remove a ten-pound tumor.

## Goal Book Bonuses

Sometimes you will receive bonuses. My sister and I have each received at least one bonus from the pictures in our Goal Books. My sister wanted the front steps and sidewalk on her house taken out and replaced with new ones. Using pictures from magazines, she constructed a nice illustration of lovely steps and a sidewalk. After the old sidewalk and steps were removed, she had to re-landscape. She and a friend drew the plans and her husband completed the actual landscaping. As a result of their renovations, they won a Beautification Award from their city.

Several months later, my sister's husband was looking through their Goal Book and noted that he hadn't realized that she had put a goal in for a Beautification Award. She said that she hadn't. However, upon looking at the goal page for the new steps and sidewalk, the photo of the house included a sign that said "Beautiful Home" that was similar to the Beautification Award sign placed in their yard. So, the award *was* in the Goal Book.

My bonus was on a page that represented a happy marriage. The photo showed a happy couple enjoying each other's company. They happened to be drinking wine from beautiful crystal glasses. That year for Christmas, my parents gave us similar crystal wine glasses, and then it became a collection with other family members contributing to complete the set. The crystal was a delightful bonus that we weren't expecting.

## Goals for Others

You cannot set goals for others. Everyone has to decide on his or her own. Even though you may feel that you know what is best for someone else, he or she must choose for him or herself. With families and couples, everyone must agree on the goals if they are family goals. If someone's goals are in conflict, you have to work it out, decide what is best for the family, or accept there will be a division in the family when the goal of an individual is granted.

This isn't "Goal Book Voodoo" where you can pick out things in other people's lives and change what you think needs to be changed. This is about each person determining what is best for him or her and wanting it to happen. Goal Books are not effective when it involves a goal that is dependent on the will of another person, such as making a person marry you, making a person give you money, or making someone give you a job. You can put a goal in your Goal Book that you want to get married—but let the universe bring you the person that would like to walk with you on the same path.

## Big Picture

When you meet your goals, you feel happy with yourself and in control of your life. When you are happy with yourself, you are happier with those around you. The opposite is true when you are not meeting your goals. When you haven't set goals and are drifting wherever life takes you, you control little in your life. And, in an effort to feel like you have some control, you might start trying to control those around you. When this happens, you start feeling less happy with everyone because they don't appreciate your trying to control their behavior. This usually results in your being overly critical of their behavior. Usually all this does is create conflict because someone didn't pick up his or her socks, or a coworker didn't give you something when you thought they should, or others are not behaving in a way you would like them to behave.

When I was working on my first Master's degree, I took a marriage and family studies class that discussed the term "Nagging Wife Syndrome." (It should actually have been termed "nagging spouse syndrome" because it can certainly be employed by either gender.) Nagging Wife Syndrome described the circumstances where women would remind their husbands of all the things they weren't doing right and then tell them how they could correct those behaviors. As I've become more experienced, I now realize that this should have been termed "Woman Not Meeting Her Goals Syndrome." I think what is really happening is the woman, in this case, is looking only at the little things in life, the to-do list that grows longer every day. She feels she has control over nothing because the to-do list that was completed yesterday looks the same as the to-do list for today. It is an endless recycling of fixing meals; washing dishes; doing laundry; picking up stuff in the house; transporting children; dealing with mail; feeding pets; watering plants; paying bills; and in most cases, going to work outside the home. It never ends and it feels like no progress is ever made in moving forward.

When we are not meeting our goals, we focus on small stuff, so that we feel like we have control over something. When we haven't identified our goals, all we have in our lives is small stuff. When we meet our goals, it frees us to look at the bigger picture and allows us to let the small things go so we enjoy life more.

When we have no goals, it is like going through life looking down at the ground; all you see is the lint on the carpeting, the weeds in the grass, the worn spots in the flooring, and the scuffs on your shoes. We become focused on such a small picture that it magnifies the imperfections. To see your goals, you have to look out into the future. It is like looking at the landscape. You see the big picture. You see the yard as a whole rather than just the weeds, or the room as a whole rather than just the lint on the carpet. It is also comparable to a hurdler running track. When they keep their eyes on the finish line, they can run more freely because they are not focusing on the hurdles.

Look out at your goals and your future, rather than focusing on the weeds and lint.

# DECIDING

*Not to decide is to decide.* My college roommate had a poster on our dorm room wall with this quote by Harvey G. Cox. I pondered it often. That is what not setting goals is about. Having no goals forces you to accept what you have now, whether you like it or not. It forces you to be a pinball; bounced around in the direction the strongest force propels you.

Some people don't make decisions because they do not know what they want. They might know what they *don't* like, but they are unable to visualize what it is they actually want.

Take a job, for example. You may know that you don't like the one you have, but you may not know enough about other jobs to determine what you do want. This is where your list helps. List the things you like to do, the things you hate to do, and the things you may not necessarily like to do but know all jobs require and you're willing to tolerate. Put a page in your Goal Book creating the feeling and mood for the things you like.

To define what you want in a job, create a list using the following statements. It helps to determine what you would like to do in a job and what you would not like to do. Choosing from the following statements may help define your goal page.

The following best describes what I would like in a job:

| | |
|---|---|
| *Like to work mostly inside* | *Like to work mostly outside* |
| *Like to work with people* | *Prefer to work alone* |
| *Like to work with the public* | *Prefer little contact with the public* |

| | |
|---|---|
| *Like to work with computers* | *Don't like to work with computers* |
| *Like to work with numbers* | *Don't like working with numbers* |
| *Like to dress up for work* | *Prefer to dress casually* |
| *Like to work with money* | *Prefer not to work with money* |
| *Like to be part of the planning* | *Prefer to be given specific tasks* |
| *Like to sell things* | *Don't like sales* |
| *Like to supervise others* | *Don't want to supervise others* |
| *Like to work with patients* | *Don't like health-related fields* |
| *Like to talk with people* | *Don't like talking with people* |
| *Like listening to people* | *Don't like listening to people* |
| *Like working with my hands* | *Don't like working with my hands* |

| | |
|---|---|
| *Like physical labor* | *Don't like physical labor* |
| *Like artistic activities* | *Don't like artistic activities* |
| *Like mechanical work* | *Don't like mechanical work* |
| *Like speaking in front of people* | *Don't like speaking in front of people* |
| *Like performing* | *Don't like to perform* |
| *Like physical activity* | *Prefer little physical activity* |
| *Like traveling* | *Do not want to travel* |

*Day trips?*

*Overnights?*

*1-5 overnights per month?*

*6-10 overnights per month?*

| | |
|---|---|
| *Like to work around food* | *Prefer not to work around food* |
| *Like to work with children* | *Prefer not to work with children* |

| | |
|---|---|
| *Like to work with animals* | *Prefer not to work with animals* |
| *Like customer-oriented work* | *Prefer not to work with customers* |
| *Like to work with the elderly* | *Prefer not to work with the elderly* |
| *Like to read* | *Prefer little reading* |
| *Like to work in a laboratory* | *Prefer not to work in a laboratory* |
| *Prefer to have my own business* | *Prefer to work for someone else* |

After you select items from this list, it will spark your thinking about other interests you have. Look at the things you would like to have as part of your job and create a goal page that represents the selected items. If you're still not sure, you could do some career exploration on the Internet or at a college career center. You may not know the name of the job you are interested in doing, but you don't have to know it. The job containing your desires will come to you. After you have created your Goal Book page, stand ready so you'll recognize the job when the universe brings it to you.

Another useful exercise is to make a list of experiences you've had on jobs that you regard as really good or really bad. Think back on bold memories at work. Even though these memories aren't entire days, usually you will remember them as a good day or a bad day at work. Make a list of the good and bad days and see what patterns emerge. You might be surprised by the similarities in each list.

I know a woman who decided to return to work when her children were in middle school and high school. She had only held a few jobs in her life, so she had little work-related experience. She had a high school education with no advanced training. She reviewed what she liked to do and what she felt she was good at doing. She had a clear vision of what she could see herself doing. She had not started actively looking for a job when she and her husband attended a social activity and met an acquaintance of her husband's who said he was looking for a dependable person to work in a particular geographic area and asked if her husband would be interested in the position. Her husband said he wasn't, but his wife might be. The man talked with my friend, explained the job, and she took it.

The job was one she never knew existed. However, she was able to recognize that she wanted the job because she had visualized the components of a job that would interest her. Had she not spent time visualizing, she might not have recognized that the universe was bringing her an opportunity when the discussion of this position came up. Her visualized goals allowed her to filter the information and reveal the aspects of this offer that matched her goals. (She found it to be an added benefit that the job paid very well.) Her visualizing and goal setting helped her land a job that was perfect for her.

## Decision-Making is Tough

The hardest part for everyone is trying to decide what he or she really wants. This isn't a skill that we are allowed to practice very often in life. Usually we are raised being told what to do and what not to do by our parents. Then we go to school where we are constantly given assignments and told to follow rules, rules, and more rules. We live in a society with an abundance of laws, rules, and social norms.

When we do make our own decisions, there are often negative consequences if our choices aren't consistent with the desires of parents, teachers, and other authoritative figures. The fear of punishment teaches us at a young age not to think too much without first getting approval. As a result, most of us never examine what we want for ourselves, much less practice thinking about it.

In talking with adults about their goals, I have made an observation regarding American culture: it seems that teens often go from being told what to do by their parents into peer relationships where they empower someone else to make decisions for them. They often do this because they are trying to please the decision-maker or because they don't want to be blamed for a decision if things don't go according to plan.

The decision-makers are put in a position where they are expected to make decisions. They may not have skills to analyze the situation or the information required to make the decision. They just make a decision because it is expected of them. As a result, most of us arrive at adulthood with few well-practiced skills for making the decisions necessary to set goals. In most cases, we have gained little practical experience for thinking through what we actually want and need. Consequently, we have a culture where many people look to others to tell them what is best for them—even when, in their own hearts, they know the decision is not taking them where they want to go. We have others making forced decisions or offering unsolicited solutions when none are requested or required.

There are, of course, exceptions. Some parents and youth-serving organizations do provide sound models for decision-making for young people to observe and practice during their developmental years.

You might need to force yourself to think through what you want and practice setting small goals until you feel confident enough to set larger goals. With the accomplishment of each goal, you will gain the experience and confidence necessary to set expanded goals.

## Choices

In the United States, we have too many choices and many of us feel overwhelmed with the task of making a decision. We are often paralyzed by the number of choices available. This is true today more than ever before in our history. Too many choices can make it difficult to make sound decisions because we often just make a choice so we can be done with it. We often feel that we don't have the information required to make decisions and we push through making a decision because one needs to be made.

We recognize that because of the way we are socialized in this country, few of us have experience making our own choices except about minor decisions. The choices we are allowed to make often have overwhelming variables, which makes the decision even more difficult. Even choosing fast food can be a daunting task. You'll notice that fast-food restaurants have recognized that customers are overwhelmed and most of them now offer a meal option so we have only to choose a number and the meal comes with pre-selected items.

Realize: there is no pressure to quickly make decisions when setting your goals. You can take all the time you need and revise your goals as often as you want. Listen to your self and focus on what is really important—then you will eliminate any choice that isn't a good match for you.

## Avoid Limits

Don't limit your goals by what you think is probable. Oftentimes when people talk about their goals, they decide not to include certain goals because they think they will never happen. Don't fall into this trap. List what you really want in your life, visualize it, make pages to represent it, and expect it to happen. My family and I would never have gone around the world if we had let logic stand in our way.

Don't talk yourself out of goals and dreams because you think they are unrealistic. If you don't nurture your hopes and dreams, I assure you, you will be disappointed. You can't hide your dreams from yourself. You can only mask them and pretend that you don't really care about them, when in your heart you know you do.

We also limit what we think we can do by what we have already done. Admit your hopes and dreams and place them in your Goal Book. Don't limit your thinking by what seems reasonable. Don't make that decision for the universe. The details are not your concern. People usually see things happening only within the framework of what is familiar to them. Let go of that traditional thinking. Many goals are realized in ways outside your imagination.

## Details

Don't get caught up in the details. Go for the broad-brush stroke. Imagine the big picture. The mood is what you are trying to visualize and then recreate on your Goal Book pages. Don't micromanage the universe. Micro-management sometimes shifts the focus from where you were originally headed. It is best to leave the details in the hands of a force greater than you; a force that can see the bigger picture.

On each page, create the mood that you want when you achieve your goal, not every little detail. You don't need to be concerned about "how your goal will be achieved" or "if you should want it" or "if you ought to have it" or "if you deserve it" or "if you're likely to get it." Just go with it. Think big. Be true to yourself and your goals. If you're in a family, be sure your goals are not in conflict with what is best for the family.

For example: Don't try to figure out solutions by writing down that you need a job to get $2,000 to pay off credit card debt so you can have a second child and work part-time. Simply put what you want: A picture of a happy woman spending time with an older child and a baby. Let the universe work out the details of how much money and how many hours you'll need to work to meet the budget. This isn't a necessary part of goal setting. After your goals are set, you simply have to trust.

When I had my first child, I was still using only words; I wasn't always fully visualizing my goals. I wanted to care for my child and not put him in day care. I was the director of a community family center and during my pregnancy, the President of the board came to me and asked (without me giving her any prompting) if I would like to bring the baby to work with me so I could care for him and still work. She pointed out that our business was caring for children two to eighteen years of age, and adding a baby to the mix would be perfectly natural. This was a solution that never crossed my mind!

My solutions were limited by my own experience, but the universe worked out the details from a broader scope. Even if I had thought of it, I would never have asked.

As my son grew older, I hired a child-care provider who came to the center and cared for him, although I was always there. This solution was a perfect balance that met my goals as a parent and my goal of having income.

When I had our second child, I wanted to leave work and stay home with the two of them, although I knew we couldn't afford it. During the sixth month of my pregnancy, I was at a meeting. During a break, I was conversing with a woman and my educational background came up. She immediately told me that she was looking for someone with that background to do some consulting work for her, and hired me on the spot.

From there a nice, flexible consulting business was born; and the business and our second son grew at about the same pace. As I had more time to do more consulting, more work came to me. We had just enough money to maintain the financial lifestyle to which we were accustomed and a work schedule that provided a comfortable harmony between my family and professional commitments.

## Goal Books Don't Guarantee Only Good in Your Life

Just because you have goals doesn't mean only good things will come to you. Life happens—and it's not always pleasant. Putting goals in your Goal Book does not ward off evil. You can visualize your core goals, but there are not goals that can block unpleasant circumstances from occurring.

Sometimes, we lose our jobs. If you have your goals in order, the next job is likely to be the one from your Goal Book. We often have to have one action to free the next action so it can occur. We may not have been brave enough to leave an unrewarding job and losing it may have seemed unbearable. That is because we can't see around the next corner where the job we envision is waiting.

I had been a CEO of a human service organization for over twenty years when I learned that there was going to be a reorganization and my job would almost certainly be eliminated. This news could have been viewed as a crushing blow, since I was still about ten years away from retirement and my age and specialized experience limited my employment opportunities. I had my goals in order, so I was able to view this as the action that was necessary to free my goals to unfold. One of my professional goals was to build a consulting business that would establish a smooth transition into a retirement job while respecting my life-long career. Another goal was to write.

As CEO, there was little latitude to establish outside consulting work because of the time commitment necessary to adhere to the professional standards of that position. As my job was slowly eliminated, it allowed for a perfect integration and I was able to relinquish the responsibilities of one job while building clientele for the next job. I had imagined many scenarios of how I could successfully create this transition and was unable to come up with one that provided the financial security that would allow me to bridge that gap while maintaining high standards in both professions. The universe worked out a seamless transition for me because I had clear pages in my Goal Book of the goals I wanted to achieve.

Life unfolds each day. Some of your goals are achieved or maintained, and other activities happen as well. In the overall picture, your goals will be achieved, even amid the chaos and uncertainty of daily living. Don't try to manage or question how the universe brings you what you want. Just accept it. Live each day and recognize your goals when they come to you.

## Summary

- Using only words to define goals often results in a literal translation.
- Using pictures to express your goals more accurately conveys the mood and condition that you have defined.
- Visualized goals using pictures have been known to produce bonuses.

- You can't set goals for other people. Everyone has to set his or her own goals.
- When we haven't set goals we are drifting and feel that we have little control over our lives.
- To feel in control, we often try to control those around us. (Bad idea.)
- When we're not meeting our larger goals, we focus on the small stuff so we feel we have control over something.
- Having no goals forces us to accept what we have now—whether we like it or not.
- Most of us never examine what we want for ourselves, much less practice thinking about it.
- Most of us arrive at adulthood with few skills necessary for making decisions required to set goals.
- We are often paralyzed by all of the choices available for making a decision.
- Don't limit your goals by what you think is probable.
- Don't talk yourself out of goals and dreams because you think they're unrealistic.
- If you don't nurture your hopes and dreams you will always be disappointed.
- Many goals are realized in ways outside our imaginations.
- Don't micro-manage the universe.
- Don't try to figure out solutions for your goals.
- After you set your goals, you simply have to trust.
- A Goal Book does not ward off evil.

# FIVE

# Staying on Track

Sometimes you will get so far off your path it can be hard to get back on. You may have to backtrack or go through some rough terrain to return. Trailblazing through rough times is very tiring.

When you are on a path that feels wrong, don't keep following it—even if you think you are on a path of no return. An example of this might be a job that you feel offers you no rewards other than a paycheck. Another example might be a relationship that you feel is suffocating your spirit. You know you're on a one-way path if every day you think about changing that aspect of your life. You may wake up each morning and wonder why you live where it is cold and overcast. You may not like anything about the house you live in. Or you may feel trapped in a relationship.

If you are on a path that you feel is one-way, think cautiously and be sure you really want to change. Moving off a one-way path is a lot like a train derailment—it causes a big mess and a lot of disruption. Eventually though, the train will run smoothly on a new track.

Make sure you're ready for a collision of goals. If you are, then set your new goal and prepare to crash. It might take some time, but the universe will soon have you back on a better course.

## Prepare and Participate

After you set your goals, you need to be prepared for when the universe brings one of your goals to you. For example, if you want to go on a trip, it is necessary to have some understanding of your destination and you need to have a tentative itinerary planned. If the destination requires a passport or visa, you will need to obtain them.

My family loves to travel, so we have four or five itineraries planned at all times so we are prepared to go when the universe reveals our destination. Achieving our goals isn't completely barrier-free just because they are in the Goal Book. We still have to actually travel the path that leads to our goals.

In my family, we participate in our goals by saving money in anticipation of those that will come to us. Out of each paycheck my husband and I pay our bills and put money away for college for our children (they have since earned their degrees), our retirement, and into a travel fund.

Some of our budgeting is for continuation goals and some of it is for event goals. Since travel is our most-loved event goal, we want to be ready for whatever trip comes to us. And, it has been amazing that the amount of money we need for each trip has always come to us. There is no particular relationship between the amount of money we have saved and the expense of the trip. Each pay period, we allocate some money to the trip fund. Regardless of the size of that fund, when the universe arranges a trip from our Goal Book it also somehow arranges for us to have the amount of money necessary for that trip. Sometimes, extra money comes to us from an unexpected place or the cost of the trip is reduced to align with the amount of money we have saved. This phenomenon has no logical explanation, but we love it!

You have to help achieve your goals. If it is your goal to write a book, you actually have to write. You can't have a goal and be a complete spectator and expect it to happen. You aren't going to wake up one morning and find a manuscript written by you on the kitchen table. You will actually have to write something. What the universe will bring to you is the inspiration to write, the time to write, and the means to publish what you've written.

If you want to go to college, you will have to apply, take required exams, apply for scholarships and financial aid, and then work to pass your classes once you are enrolled. The universe will clear a path; it is you who must walk to your goal.

Once you have defined your goals, you must have the expectation that your goals will come to you.

We prepared for a vacation to Asia for many years before the universe arranged a trip for us. From the time our children were preschoolers, we talked about the foods and cultures of Asian countries, we used chopsticks when we ate Asian foods, and we read books about the people in various Asian countries. Sure enough, on our first trip to China, we went into a restaurant and even our children were ready to meet the challenge of our achieved goal.

We had dreamed it, we had visualized it, we had prepared for it, we had expected it, and finally we lived it.

## Watch for Clues

Each day is filled with choices that help you move toward or away from your goals. Sometimes it's difficult to tell what choice to make because it can be unclear as to which direction each choice will lead. This is when you watch for clues. They are almost always there, although they are sometimes hard to see.

Clearly defined goals serve as filters for everything you see and do. Everything that happens around you is strained through a goal-filter, sorting out what is part of your goal and what is not. Without goals, valuable treasures can be washed past you because you don't realize you should be watching for them.

I worked with a woman who put in her Goal Book that she wanted to own a Jeep. She wanted a green Jeep with a tan roof and it needed to be in her price range. She looked at used car lots and couldn't find one that met her needs. She was looking in the classified ads one day and saw an advertisement for a Jeep that seemed to be the right price, although the ad gave no information on color. She arranged to look at the vehicle and it was the exact green and tan color combination she wanted. When she looked inside, she saw her clue. The floor mats were of a cartoon character that was one of her favorites and matched a magnet that she always kept on her refrigerator. She bought the Jeep and has been delighted with it.

I knew another woman who put in her Goal Book that she wanted to live in a log cabin on a lake. While looking for a place to live, she answered an ad that was for a log cabin on a lake. The landlord negotiated the price so it was in her range and she could afford it. When she looked at the cabin, she was immediately met with her clue: a painting on the wall that was her favorite, exactly like one she had. This was the clue she needed to help her realize she was in the cabin she had visualized. She moved in and enjoyed the realization of her goal.

# IT DOESN'T ALWAYS HAPPEN THE WAY YOU IMAGINE

When I was a teenager, I had a goal, although it seemed more like a fantasy. My front teeth were spread apart and I spoke with a lisp. By the time I was in high school, I was self-conscious about my speech and wished the lisp would go away. I learned to carefully choose my words so I used as few words as possible that started with the letter "s." I wanted to speak clearly and have teeth without gaps. I knew there was no way that my dream could come true, but I often visualized how I would look and imagined speaking without a lisp. I didn't realize that braces could help my teeth because I had never known anyone with braces. I had seen them on a child in a television show, but that wasn't real to me and I certainly never imagined having them on my teeth. I also didn't know there was a connection between my teeth and my lisp. I wanted to be rescued. I wanted a fairy godmother to come along and touch me with her magic wand and make my teeth and speech the way I wanted them.

I had a lucky break while I was away at college. I broke a molar. It was a bad break around a large filling. It hurt and I needed to have it repaired sooner rather than later. The university I attended was several hours from home and my parents advised me to find a dentist in the town where I was living to have it repaired. I found a dentist. When he looked into my mouth he said that I needed braces, speech therapy, and I would have to relearn to swallow. He told me that I had a tongue-thrust and every time I swallowed it contributed to separating my teeth. He also told me that the tongue-thrust contributed to my lisp. He advised me that these things needed to be corrected or my teeth would erode as I aged.

This was the beginning of a dream come true by way of a nightmare! Having braces and speech therapy is common today, although it was rare for someone growing up in rural America in the 1970s. I had braces on my teeth during most of my college years. At that time, I felt like I was the only twenty-year-old on the planet who was wearing braces. I also spent all four years of college in speech therapy, a humbling experience to say the least.

Finally, my goal, my fantasy, my wildest impossible dream was realized! I had straight teeth and I could speak without a lisp! It didn't happen the easy way with a fairy godmother. It happened because I remembered every day that it was my goal and I worked on my speech every day after the universe showed me the path I needed to follow.

If I had not had the goal of straight teeth and speaking without a lisp, the news about braces and speech therapy would have seemed a disaster. Since I had my goals in place, however, I was able to see the long road of speech correction for the dream come true it was rather than a social disaster for a college student. Sometimes, even now, when I am really tired or under great pressure, my tongue becomes lazy and a little lisp sneaks out. I know that it's a reminder from the universe to help me remember that **dreams with attitude make goals happen**.

## Never Give Up

Goals won't always come to you on your timetable and it is easy to give up and assume that a particular goal will never be achieved. Well, never give up because your goals know their own time. When you set deadlines it is an attempt to impose your will on the universe. When you remove deadlines, you remove the possibility of failure. You are left with "goals achieved" and "goals not yet achieved." When the universe doesn't function to meet your deadlines, you tend to declare that your goal is a failure because it didn't meet your expected timetable. Oftentimes the universe is busy helping you meet goals that require more immediate achievement. Goals, like the births of children, know their own time.

# Conflicting Goals

Conflicting goals are goals that cannot be successful if they exist at the same time. The fewer connections a person has to other people or things, the fewer opportunities there are for conflict. If you are traveling through life solo, your conflicting goals are limited to conflicts that involve only you. Examples of conflicting goals might be that you would like to be thin and you would like to eat freely. You may want to be fit, yet not want to exercise. In these instances, you can have each of the conflicting goals, just not at the same time. You will have to decide which is most important to you and put that one in your Goal Book.

Even a Goal Book can't defy the laws of nature and make it possible to be fit while never moving a muscle. It could allow you to be thin and eat everything you wanted; however, it may involve a metabolic disorder! If you have a goal of working in a certain job that requires you to arrive early in the morning, rested and ready for work, and you also have the goal of staying up late at night partying with friends, well, then you have conflicting goals. If you are unable to decide which is most important, your behavior may dominate the issue and create the situation where you are forced to choose.

Personal conflicting goals don't stay in conflict very long because your behavior usually reveals the dominant goal; unless you make a conscious decision to focus on the less dominate one.

As soon as you start adding components to your life, you have an increased possibility for conflict. If you are single and add a house, then there is a potential conflict if another goal involves moving to a new location. A house inspires many conflicting goals if your vision doesn't involve yard work, maintenance, and repair. If you add a pet to the mix, the conflicts increase if you have travel as a goal. So, it is important to look at your goals and determine if they are in conflict. If they are, put in the goal you want now and add the other goal when you are ready for it to be achieved. And, for every human relationship you add to your life, you add joy, sorrow, and conflicting goals.

You may have conflicting goals and not know it. I had conflicting goals between my need for work, my desire for family time, and my professional aspirations. I wanted to write a book and earn money so I could leave my job and spend more time with my children. I was also meddling with details rather than letting the universe prevail. I wanted security, flexibility, time with my family, and a stable income. My job offered security, stable income, and flexible work hours so I could have time with my family. I never really appreciated it because I felt that I wasn't reaching my professional goal of writing, consulting, and helping a broader group of people develop life-management skills. I marked each birthday as a measure of the time I had lost in meeting my professional goals. What I didn't recognize is that I was successfully reaching my personal goal of spending time with my family as well as some of my professional goals.

Our sphere of influence is really quite limited, although we might think we influence many people around us. I was reaching my most important personal goal by providing the most influence over my children's lives during their developmental years when they were most impressionable. I was able to do this by spending quantities of time with them because my job allowed me to have the flexibility to do this. Even though my job didn't fulfill all of my professional goals, I was fulfilling my personal goals. Since I had conflicting goals, the most important one was met at the time it needed to be met. Now I have time and energy to devote to my other professional goals. If I had tried to write this book earlier, first, I didn't have the experience necessary to write it; and second, I would have neglected my children—and that would have been in direct conflict with one of my most important core goals.

It has been my experience that core and continuation goals

usually dominated when I had to make decisions about conflicting event goals. The favorite job of my career was working for a university in its Extension Program providing marriage and family outreach services. I loved everything about that job. I think I would have enjoyed it forever. The first conflict came after I married and my husband didn't find a job near my place of employment. I decided to leave my beloved job, thinking that I would always have the opportunity to return. My core goal of happiness and my continuation goal of maintaining a stable marriage with two incomes prevailed over my event goal of a job.

I maintained contact with my supervisor and waited for an opening to come along, so I could return. Sure enough, an opening occurred in a location where both Chuck and I wanted to relocate. I was at another crossroads. This time, I had just given birth to our second son and my core goals and continuation goals dominated again. I would not let go of my commitment to care for our sons, so I did not accept the position I desired.

Review where you are in your life and ask yourself if you have conflicting goals. One example is if you want to have a lot of money *but* you don't want to work much. Or, you might want to spend a lot of time away from home with your friends *and* make a commitment to fulfilling obligations to a marriage and family. Or, you may want to finish a degree *and* spend time traveling extensively. These goals are in conflict if you expect to have them at the same time.

You can achieve goals that appear to be in conflict, but you have to choose which one you want right now. Remember, *put only those goals in your Goal Book that you are prepared for now.* You can have all of them, just perhaps not successfully at the same time.

Goal achievement comes at different times in your life. When goals are in conflict, it's simply the wrong time for that goal to be achieved. Instead of being disappointed, just realize that you have a lifetime. Relax. Many of your continuation goals change in intensity as time passes.

Parenting, for example, is intense for the first few years and then the time commitment has various peaks and valleys until the children are about eighteen to twenty. Over a lifetime, that's a relatively short period to parent and you don't get a second chance to get it right. A job can be intense when you are first learning it, then as time passes and you become more experienced, the intensity decreases. As this intensity decreases, you have time for more goals to be introduced and achieved.

Life is a continuous balance between the intensity of each of your goals. You will feel harmony when you accept this delicate balance and allow your goals to be integrated with each other. You can have it all, just not at the same time. Let time be your friend. Your goals will come to you when the time is right.

## Summary

- When you get off-track, it can be difficult to get back on.
- After you set your goals, you need to be prepared for the time when the universe brings one of your goals to you.
- You have to help achieve your goals.
- Each day is filled with choices that help move you toward or away from your goals.
- Goals serve as filters for sorting daily information to determine what is part of your goal.
- Goals don't happen on your timetable.
- Never give up and assume you won't reach a goal.
- When you remove deadlines from your goals, you remove the possibility of failure.

- Conflicting goals are goals that could not be successful if they existed at the same time.
- As you add relationships to your life, you add the potential for joy, sorrow, and conflicting goals.
- Life is a continuous balance between the intensity of each of your goals.
- Goals can come in any order. Put only those goals in your Goal Book that you are prepared to achieve right now.
- You will feel harmony in your life when you accept the delicate balance and integration between your goals.
- You can have it all, just not at the same time.

# SIX

# Life Stages

People can begin to set goals for themselves as soon as they reach the "age of reason," which is about seven years old. The first goals for children are often simple and usually consist of concrete objects, such as wanting a toy or a book. As the child grows into adolescence and is able to think abstractly, then more complex goals can be visualized.

Everyone's life is composed of many stages and it is important to update your Goal Book as you prepare for each of them. You can recognize major life stages because they appear as crossroads that alter your current patterns of behavior. Some of the major stages include:

- Choosing a career
- Choosing a job
- Going to college
- Getting married

- ◆ Maintaining a marriage
- ◆ Having a child
- ◆ Getting a divorce
- ◆ Retiring from a job
- ◆ Changing jobs
- ◆ Parenting a child
- ◆ Buying a house
- ◆ Becoming a grandparent

All of these stages can occur once or multiple times in any one person's life. It is important to recognize when these changes are on the horizon and prepare for them before you are actually at a crossroads with no goals to guide you.

It is also useful to examine your goals after major life events such as a divorce or the death of a loved one. It can be stabilizing to look at your Goal Book and congratulate yourself on where you have been. It can be healing to then set goals and visualize where you want to go. When major life events occur, a feeling of chaos usually follows. Setting goals is a way of calming the chaos and restoring a sense of order to your life.

I will discuss four of these continuation life stages because they are central in most people's lives. Career, marriage, parenthood, and retirement are significant life-altering changes that, without proper planning, can be disastrous for the participants. All of these life stages begin as event goals and graduate into continuation goals. They are stages that will affect you for long periods of time and your planning, or lack thereof, seeps into the lives of others. I will begin by discussing career choices.

## Career

A career is something that is generally chosen during your early adult life. A career is something you do regardless of the job you have. A career is the goal you set for yourself regarding what you want to accomplish in life. This accomplishment will be completed over the course of many jobs. Jobs are what you do to earn money. A career is what you do to follow your passion.

This may seem a bit confusing. I'll use the example of my father. He held many jobs throughout his life. He held jobs as a stonemason and bricklayer, a general contractor, and owner of a construction company. Those titles are the ways he earned money to support his family. He chose the jobs because he loved the work. The common thread through all of those jobs is his career. I believe his career was to teach young men to have a strong work ethic and realize their responsibilities to their families. He provided extra work whenever one of his employees needed extra money, he counseled them regarding their family responsibilities, and provided them with encouragement and support when they needed it.

Jobs provide you with money, your *career* is a clear vision of what you hope to accomplish while you are in this world.

Generally, when people choose a job path, they choose work they can enjoy. When deciding on a career, think of what you would like to accomplish in this world. What is your goal for the career of your life? What do you feel passionate about? Next, think of what work you enjoy doing and how you will fit enjoyable work into your career. People usually define their careers by their work. Instead, we should define our work by our careers; because we can always work on our career goal regardless of the job we are doing.

Both of my sons ran cross-country in high school. There is a lot of time spent waiting to run and a lot of time spent riding a school bus to get to the meets. My youngest son discovered the career of the bus driver. This man drove a bus for his job, but his career was encouraging teenagers to do their best. He spent time talking with the runners and encouraged them when they didn't feel they had done their best or when they were too tired to try. There was a cut in school funding and his job as bus driver was eliminated. He continued his career (of counseling teenagers) by volunteering to drive the bus. The man who drove the bus continues to be an inspiration in my son's life, and the lives of many to whom he regularly provides encouragement.

I have a friend who has worked as a college professor, a program director for university Extension Programs, and is now retired from those positions. Her jobs have always been related to increasing knowledge and improving the lives of families and individuals through education. I have known her for thirty years, and I believe her career is that of inspiring, nurturing, and mentoring women in their professional development. Each time I talk with her or receive a card from her, she always nurtures my professionalism. She isn't paid to do this. It is not in her job description. She shares inspirational stories about other women and their professionalism and role-models her commitment to professionalism.

When we meet, she asks about my career and my professional development before ever sharing stories or trials of her life. No one asks her to do these things, no one instructs her to do them. It is her passion. It is her career. It is one of her core goals and I'm sure she will continue to pursue this passion her entire life.

I have a friend who worked as an investment advisor. He defined his career as helping people manage their money so they could more effectively reach their life goals. In this instance, his career and his job were consistent. His career, however, reached far beyond the confines of his job. He volunteered time with his church and with various nonprofit organizations to teach money management to many people who would never have had enough money to invest at his firm. He continued his career of helping people manage their money long after he retired from his job.

I have found that career goals are generally part of your core goals. They are not event goals. Jobs are event goals. People who have defined their career goals are very clear about them. They never tire of their career goals, although they may tire of their jobs. They continue in their career goals regardless of what job they may hold or whether they are retired from a job. They never have to be told to do their career goals. They awaken each morning with excitement, anxious to embrace their careers.

- Defining your career goal defines the purpose of your existence.
- When major life events occur, a feeling of chaos usually follows.
- Setting goals is a way of calming the chaos and restoring a sense of order to your life.
- A career is something you do regardless of the job you have.
- Jobs are what you do to earn money.
- A career is what you do to reach a goal.
- Your career is a clear vision of what you hope to accomplish while you are in this world.
- People usually define their careers by their work. We should, instead, define our work by our careers.

## MARRIAGE

In researching the origin of marriage, it appears that marriage came about in response to the conception of a child. When the couple became aware there was a child on the way, they set the goal for themselves and made a commitment to their social group to care for the child since it was completely dependent. Another part of their commitment was to raise their child and teach him or her the skills necessary for adulthood in their culture. Even though they didn't have a Goal Book, they began approaching the future with that goal as their guide.

Today, the goal of marriage has radically shifted its focus. Marriage and pregnancy are no longer directly linked. Because of this, I will discuss goal setting for couples and for parents separately. I will define couples as any two people who have committed to travel the path of life together and parents as those couples or singles who have set the goal of having children and then teaching these children the skills necessary to be successful adults in their culture. I will discuss goal setting for all couples in general and then discuss the specifics of goal setting for parents.

When you form a relationship as a couple and begin to think about traveling into the future together, that is when you need to sit down together and generate a list for your Goal Book. I suggest that you do this as soon as the idea of "being together for a long time" comes into your heads. Start by having each partner make a list of where he or she would like to be in five to ten years. After you make your individual lists, compare them and start creating your Goal Book pages. Remember, a written list can be misleading to the universe, so once your goals are established, illustrate them and place the pages in your Goal Book.

Here is an example of a list that might be generated by a couple.

In five to ten years, I would like the following things to be true in my life:

| **Man** | **Woman** |
|---|---|
| *A place of our own* | *A place of our own* |
| *Friends to spend time with* | *Friends to spend time with* |
| *A vacation at least once a year* | *A vacation at least once a year* |
| *A good job* | *A good job* |
| *Time to relax* | *Time to relax* |

It looks like this couple is a perfect match! They both want exactly the same things in life. Once they start illustrating their Goal Book, they will share more clearly what their words mean. In reality, to the man "a place of our own" means an apartment in the city with absolutely no yard work because he hates yard work and loves the city. The woman wants a house in the country with a large lawn and lots of gardens. The "perfect match" paints their pictures very differently.

Likewise, "Friends to spend time with," can have a variety of meanings. The man may illustrate this concept showing other male friends watching sporting events on television, while the woman may illustrate this concept as having couples over for dinner. A vacation for one may mean a rustic fishing trip in the wild, while the other partner may expect a pampered cruise. A "good job" for one might mean working the afternoon shift so he or she doesn't have to get up early; while for the other it may mean making a certain amount of money. "Time to relax" could mean anything from watching television, golfing, or doing the dreaded yard work.

I encourage you to always make the visual goal pages to avoid misunderstandings. Visualizations are worth a thousand words.

If your lists and goal pages don't have much in common, maybe the relationship isn't a good match. Maybe you are traveling different paths and it is best to part ways. The more you struggle to make another person travel on the path you've chosen and the more they struggle to get to their own path, the more conflict the relationship has—until each of you is free to travel on the paths that lead to your individual goals.

When you have conflicting goals with a partner or spouse, one of you is always dominating and pulling the other one toward a goal. The person being pulled is always resistant if they are not interested in being a part of that particular goal.

We've all seen couples with opposing goals trying to travel together through life. They are two people who struggle down a path, dragging each other back and forth as they try to reach their individual goals. Finally, after much conflict and pain, they realize they are not traveling on the same paths and separate so they can move toward their individual goals.

It spares couples a lot of pain when they acknowledge early that a relationship simply isn't a good match. If your goals are not aligned, your life together will not be in alignment either. As painful as it may seem, it is best to give it up and look for someone who will joyfully travel with you on the same path, seeking the same goals that you seek.

When you set goals as a couple, it can be useful to discuss your goals within the context of creating a Goal Book. Using a Goal Book as a tool to discuss the future allows individuals within the partnership to freely talk about their goals. It allows the couple to discuss goals more objectively. It removes the personal attachment and allows the couple to talk about goals as something separate from themselves and to voice their thoughts on why they may or may not be interested in a goal. It allows each person the freedom to discuss the other person's goals and then embrace, modify, or reject the idea of the goal without rejecting the other person.

When couples disagree over issues, they are often actually disagreeing about their goals. By using a Goal Book, it allows the couple to recognize that it is their commitment to each other's goals that may be in conflict, not their commitment to each other. It allows their attachment to each other and their conflicting goals to co-exist.

Goal conflict is usually a disagreement about the level of priority that each person places on a goal. The only way to remove the goal from conflict is to discuss the level of commitment that each person has to the goal at that time.

An example might be that the man has a goal to buy a boat and the woman has a goal to buy new carpeting. They may agree that a boat and carpeting are goals that they would both like to achieve. In this instance, the problem is timing. If both goals are placed in the Goal Book, one member of the couple might *nudge* the universe and buy the item because it was in the Goal Book. Before this happens, the couple needs to talk about the goals and decide if one is more critical than the other. The more critical item is the one that goes in the Goal Book because the couple is ready for it to be achieved at this time. The other goal can be placed in the Goal Book when it is a priority.

I have known couples who have chosen the boat as the first priority and couples who have chosen the carpeting. I have also known couples who have chosen to put both goals in their Goal Book and agreed to allow their goals to filter the opportunities brought to them by the universe.

Compare your lists and the visions of your goals. If you discover that some of your goals are in conflict, you will need to discuss what is important now and what can be put in the Goal Book later. You can negotiate and decide which goals are most important to the marriage, which are in conflict with the well-being of the marriage, and which individual goals can exist in harmony with the marriage.

I think you will find that many individual goals can exist in harmony with the goals of the marriage. If you feel your goals can exist in harmony, you may place all of them in your Goal Book and the universe will prioritize them for you.

If you believe in your commitment to another person, then the first priority is to keep the marriage/relationship alive and serve the goals that are best for it. It is no longer a matter of "what I want."

If you are married and your first priority is a goal other than advancing the goals of the marriage/relationship and doing what is best to achieve those goals, then marriage or that relationship may not be one of your goals. Agreeing on the goals that should be placed in a Goal Book is agreeing to accept those goals as the universe brings them to you.

Think about this, if your wedding day is the best day of your life, you have already determined that you will have thousands of days together that will never be as happy. Change that outlook with your Goal Book and make the best yet to come!

### Some guidelines for setting goals as a couple:

- If the goal of both individuals is to stay together, you need to generate your list of goals together.
- If your lists have nothing in common, it is best to cut your losses and find someone else.
- Visualize your goals and compare visions.
- Don't try to convince your partner that your goals are the better goals.
- If your goals are different, see if they can exist together and be compatible.
- Everyone's goal for a happy marriage/relationship will look different. The important thing is that it looks the same for the partners in the marriage/relationship.
- Couples can have different goals as long as they are not conflicting or at cross-purposes.
- Before placing goals in your Goal Book, you both need to agree on them and be comfortable wanting them to come to you.
- This is not Goal Book Voodoo. You can't put in desired changes about your partner; even if everyone you know agrees that it is in his or her best interest.
- Revisit your joint goals. Update them as circumstances change in your lives.
- Successful couples need to look into the future through the same eyes.

- Using a Goal Book allows couples to recognize that their commitment to each other's goals can be in conflict while their commitment to each other can remain intact.
- Goal conflict is often a *goal priority* conflict.
- Often the woman in the couple does most of the actual construction of the Goal Book. That's okay, as long as there is equal participation by both partners in generating the goal list and visualizing how each goal looks.
- If you hear yourself saying, "My spouse will kill me if I tell him/her I did this (or bought this)," you can be sure that you have just deviated from an agreed upon goal within your marriage.

## Parenthood

It is important for a couple to discuss and visualize their goals for having children long before conception or adoption. It is possible that one of the partners may not be interested in having children or may be interested in postponing childbearing until a later date. When you choose to become a parent, you're a parent for life. There's no turning back. Even if you give the child up for adoption or leave the child in the care of others while you seek alternative goals, you are still a parent. Your life is altered forever.

Deciding to be a parent should *be a decision* and you should enter with caution. It can be like changing your mind after you've entered one of those parking lots with toothed grates that allow you to enter but claw into your tires if you attempt to exit. If you choose to turn back, it ruins your tires. With a child, if you decide to turn back, it may result in devastating consequences for the child's life. And yours.

If you decide that parenting is one of your goals, it is important to define child-rearing goals through visualization if your parenting is to be successful. Here are a few questions to help you get started:

- Do both of you want to have a child?
- If you do want a child, when would you like to have one?
- Do you envision putting the child in day care?
- Do you envision full- or part-time day care?
- Do you envision that both parents will work full-time after the birth or adoption of your child?
- What is your vision of caring for the child?
- What is your vision of your spouse's responsibility in caring for the child? (This needs to be answered by each parent individually.)
- What is your vision of how a child should be disciplined?
- What is your vision of how a child should be educated?
- What do you see as your life-long responsibility as a parent?

Discussing these questions, visualizing them, and preparing a corresponding Goal Book page will eliminate much of the confusion of parenting responsibility. Often couples visualize the birth of the child and then skip to a vision of playing catch in the front yard and completely miss creating the continuation goals necessary to visualize the day-to-day management of parenting. Providing daily care for a child takes a tremendous amount of time, in addition to your other daily tasks. Without careful visualization and goal setting, the responsibilities of parenting can take many adults by surprise.

Be prepared to rework your goal page(s) about parenting soon after your child is born. As a parent, you see the world differently than you did as a non-parent. No one can explain this to you before the birth of your child. It remains for me the greatest wonder of the world.

If you decide you want to be a parent, you may want to spend a lot of time on these pages. (If there are two parents, these pages need to be visualized together.) There are many reasons for deciding to have a child, but there is really only one goal in parenting: to raise a child so that he or she is prepared to function as an adult with the skills necessary to succeed in this world. Essentially, you are deciding to be responsible for the future of the world! You are agreeing to do this without training, without support, without guidance, with no education for the task, and usually in isolation.

Becoming a parent can be an ill-fated idea without carefully setting and visualizing goals. Raising a child under these circumstances is a little bit like being expected to build a car without having a current working model to copy. Just because you've ridden in cars doesn't mean you have a clue how to build one. The same is true with raising children. Successful child rearing doesn't just happen, as so many may assume. It requires a great deal of visualization to set the continuation goal of parenting. It also requires frequent discussions between parents to be sure both still agree on the vision they created and placed in their Goal Book.

## Creating an Environment for Nurturing Children

Parenting continuation goals are the most complex. We've already determined that you can't set goals for others—although for a period of time, parenting is the exception. Children reach the age of reason when they are about seven. This is when they can see cause-and-effect relationships and begin visualizing their futures.

Therefore, for the first seven years of their lives, it is necessary for parents to set goals for their children. This is complicated because it is actually accomplished by parents setting goals for themselves. Imagine that children are magnets. As a parent, you create an environment filled with qualities that you want to cling to your little magnets. Children are born with certain characteristics and then they add to their original makeup whatever is in their environment. Children reach adulthood cluttered with characteristics, habits, sayings, attitudes, and ideas that have clung to them as they grew up.

When creating your parenting goal pages, think about what you will need to create the environment necessary to raise the child you want to have. Imagine your child as an adult and visualize the qualities you want him or her to possess. Think about what your role will be in creating those desired qualities. As a parent, what goals must you have for yourself to create the environment filled with the characteristics that you want to be clinging to your child when he or she becomes an adult? If you want your children to do well in school, what is your part in creating that success? What does your family look like during this stage?

We often spend a lot of time discussing and shopping for the physical environment of a baby's room. We look at color schemes, animal themes, furniture types, and wall color. A Goal Book gives you the opportunity to spend as much time visualizing your child's learning environment as you do visualizing his or her physical environment. Give their environment for development as much thought as you give the color scheme of their room.

I once heard a story that was said to be about Mahatma Gandhi. Whether it is accurate or not, I can't be sure, but I think you'll enjoy it. As the story was told to me, a woman who lived in India had a son who was about ten years old. They lived in a remote village and had little access to health and dental care. They were also very poor and could not afford dental care. Her son was old enough to go out on his own, and he discovered refined sugar and loved the taste of it. He ate candy and chewed gum; and as a result, his teeth were decaying. His mother was concerned for the health of his teeth and told him to stop eating sugar. He liked eating sugar and continued to do so despite his mother's objections. His mother felt that he would listen to Gandhi if Gandhi told him to stop eating sugar because Gandhi was such a well-respected person in India. The mother packed up her son and traveled quite a distance to meet with Mr. Gandhi. She requested that Mr. Gandhi instruct her son to stop eating sugar. Gandhi asked her to bring her son back in six weeks. Puzzled by this request, she agreed and in six weeks, the mother and son made the trip back to meet with Mr. Gandhi.

Mr. Gandhi looked at the boy and told him to stop eating sugar because the habit caused his mother great distress. He explained that the distress came because they had little money to pay for dental care and they lived far from anyone who could care for his teeth. He told the boy his teeth needed to last his lifetime and he should heed his mother's advice and stop eating sugar. The boy understood and agreed that he would stop eating sugar.

The mother was confused and frustrated. She asked Mr. Gandhi why he couldn't have told her son to stop eating sugar six weeks earlier when they were there. She said it would have saved them the long return trip. Mr. Gandhi replied that six weeks ago, he was eating sugar.

The point is: we can't expect more from our children than we expect from ourselves. As Gandhi said, "You must be the change you want to see in the world." This applies to most behavior, including parenting. We must visualize our children as we want them to be as adults and create goals for ourselves as parents to be the change we hope to see in our children.

I'm sure you have played the game Simon Says. As you recall, the person playing the part of Simon gives an instruction for the group to do a certain action while performing that same action himself. Simon might say, "Simon says, touch your ear." The other people in the game are to do things only when Simon says to do them. The trick comes when Simon does an action and doesn't preface it with the words "Simon says." Many of the players do the activity that Simon demonstrates and they are eliminated from the game.

Parenting is a lot like Simon Says. Children are much better at doing what they see rather than doing what we tell them to do. Transferring information to children almost always results in "what *they* see is what *you* get." This is why visualizing your role as a parent and setting parenting goals for yourself is critical in determining goals for how you want your children to be when they are adults. Parenting is a commingling of souls; and as parents, you actually have to "be the change you want to see . . ."

As your children grow, continue to update your Goal Book pages. It is easy to feel pressured to do what "all the other parents" are doing. If all of your friends use a certain day care, it's easy to join the group. Later, it may be popular for children to join soccer or dance and you may feel compelled to have your child join, too. With each stage of your child's development, evaluate your goals and the environment *you* want for your child. Don't allow yourself to be pulled away from your goals to follow the popular trends embraced by other parents. Look at your Goal Book pages often and refresh your memory on where you are going and why. When you look at your goals, you will gather strength for reaching them.

Here is a list of qualities that many parents agree they would like their children to possess if they are to be successful adults. This list, although not comprehensive, may help you generate ideas for your parenting goals.

**When my children are adults, I would like them to:**

- Contribute to society by helping others
- Be loving and kind
- Have good nutrition habits by eating healthy meals
- Have good table manners
- Understand effective communication between adults
- Understand problem-solving skills to solve conflicts as they arise in life

- Understand positive interactions between spouses and other adults
- Have been protected from child abuse and sexual abuse
- Understand the world from a global perspective
- Have an appreciation of other cultures by celebrating other cultures
- Understand social injustices as they occur in the world
- Have good social skills
- Have practical skills such as home repair, clothing repair, car maintenance, food preparation, laundry skills, and various other necessary living skills
- Have organizational skills
- Be able to clean and maintain a home, yard, and vehicle
- Have the ability to earn a living
- Be capable of successfully coping in and contributing to society
- Be capable of forming lasting attachments to others
- Have the skills necessary to be successful adults:
    - effective communication skills
    - sharing
    - work ethic
    - honesty
    - fairness
    - cooperation

When creating pages for parenting, think through all of the questions about having children and the physical care aspects that I outlined at the beginning of this section and create pages that represent the continuation goals that follow the birth of each child. Then spend time discussing the qualities you want your child to possess when he or she is an adult and create a continuation page(s) showing your part in creating the environment necessary to develop the qualities you envision. Evaluate your pages often, update them as your family changes, look at your Goal Book pages regularly, and enjoy your child as he or she grows into the person you envisioned.

- Becoming a parent should actually be a decision that you have set as a goal.
- When creating your parenting goal pages, think about what you will need to create the environment necessary to raise your child.
- A Goal Book gives you the opportunity to spend as much time visualizing your child's learning environment as you do visualizing his or her physical environment.
- Keep updating your Goal Book pages as your child grows.
- As children grow, parents need to continually discuss their parenting goals to be sure they still share the same parenting vision.
- Look at your Goal Book often and refresh your memory on where you are going and why. (If there are two parents, this should be done together.)
- When you look at your goals, you will gather strength for reaching them.
- Choose pictures for your Goal Book that represent the family life that you desire.
- Be the change you wish to see in your child.

## Retirement

With a Goal Book, you can continue to set goals and have a meaningful life regardless of your age. Often the last goal we set for ourselves is the event goal of retiring from a job. And, too often when we set the goal of retirement, we set only the event goal of leaving our job. We give very little consideration to the years that follow, which are really a continuation goal.

Some people have a long to-do list of tasks they didn't have time to complete while they were employed. Others have a list of travel destinations. These two lists are the extent of most retirement planning.

When people have completed their lists, sometimes they have included items such as continuing their education or starting a long-term project. Then they will say that it's too late in their lives to start something that will take so long. They give the excuse of age and point out that they'll be sixty-eight or seventy-five by the time they complete the project. Well, with any luck, they'll be sixty-eight or seventy-five either way, with or without accomplishing their goal.

In this day and age, retirement can last a long time. My grandparents were actively retired and remained in good health for over twenty years. That's longer than most of us spend in one job during our working years. Retirement is a time when it is dangerously tempting to become a pinball; allowing yourself to be thrust in different directions by outside forces. Visualizing retirement and creating Goal Book pages is a critical step in preserving the quality and productivity of those precious years.

As you prepare to create your Goal Book pages, consider the following question. *What do you want your retirement to look like?* It is important to think about this long before you reach retirement age. When you enter retirement, just like the other stages in your life, you probably know what you want to retire *from*.

- I don't want to get up early every day if I feel like sleeping in.
- I don't want the demands that come with full-time employment.
- I don't want deadlines.

- I don't want daily rush-hour driving.
- I don't want to be exhausted by hundreds of demands.

These are some of the pressures of employment that we gladly want to leave behind.

Most of us also know that we don't want to retire into the following situations:

- I don't want to spend retirement sitting alone.
- I don't want to spend retirement doing nothing.
- I don't want to spend retirement parenting grandchildren.
- I don't want to spend all of my time caring for elderly parents.
- I don't want to spend all of my time watching television.

A few people preparing for the continuation goal of retirement do get as far as loosely defining things they would like to do in their retirement years.

- I want to go someplace warm in the winter.
- I want to have time to read.
- I want to have time to play golf and fish.
- I want to have time to garden.
- I want to have time for hobbies.
- I want time to get organized.

When preparing your Goal Book pages, go back to Chapter 2 and start with a list. I hear people who are nearing retirement say they want time to do what they want to do. Without goals and visualizations, days slip away and soon years are gone without doing what they wanted to do. Generate your list by answering the following questions and visualizing how each would look:

- Imagine the perfect day without "have-to-do's." What would it look like?
- How many days do you want like that?
- Do you want to travel? Where?
- How do you want to travel? By plane, train, ship, or car? Do you want to lodge in a camper, tent, motel, or condo? Do you want long-term stays or short-term trips?
- Do you want to visit national parks, museums, cities, or other countries?
- What do you want to accomplish?
- Do you want more time to fish, hunt, read, or write?
- Do you want to spend more time with family and friends?
- Do you want to join the Peace Corps?
- Do you want to research your family's genealogy?
- Do you want to take college courses?
- Do you want to take classes while you travel through Elderhostel? (www.elderhostel.org)
- Do you want time to pursue hobbies that have been on hold or work in your garden?
- Do you want to learn to play a musical instrument or act in a play?
- Do you want to volunteer for a nonprofit or a school?
- Do you want to complete those scrapbooks and photo albums that you've never had time to finish?
- Do you want to learn a foreign language or teach a class?
- Do you want to start a business?
- Would you like to write down family stories or a family history of your family's events to pass on to children and grandchildren?

- Would you like to copy family photos and make albums for younger family members?
- Would you like to work in a field of interest where you were never employed?
- Would you like to do some consulting work and share the expertise developed from years of experience?
- Do you what to share your expertise by mentoring a young person in your field?
- Do you want to spend time with a child to help create "the change you want to see in the world"?
- Do you want to spend time with the elderly?
- Would you like to volunteer for hospice?
- Would you like to continue to work part-time in your current job?
- Would you like to go on an archeological dig?
- Would you like to learn to cook foreign cuisine?
- Would you like to tutor a child or young person?
- Would you like to visit every state in the United States?
- Would you like to visit every continent?
- Would you like to visit all of the countries of a certain continent?
- Would you like to visit every province in Canada?
- Would you like to wade in every ocean or swim in all of the Great Lakes?

I encourage you to put all of your goals in your Goal Book, regardless of your age. Meeting a goal is timeless. It's not as if goals have expiration dates and must be discarded like a gallon of sour milk. Continue to live your dreams.

I have a great-aunt and great-uncle, both of whom completed their requirements for high school graduation and finally graduated when they were in their seventies! They did it together and were very proud of their accomplishments. (We were proud of them, too.)

I have a friend who worked at a college where an eighty-five-year-old woman completed her Bachelor's degree. The eighty-five-year-old said no one in her family had ever graduated from college and she felt she needed to be a role-model for the younger generations. She not only graduated, but she did so with honors because she expected nothing less from her children and grandchildren. She was the "the change she wanted to see" in her family.

I know a married couple who planned carefully for their retirements. They examined all of their options and then set clear goals for themselves. They enjoy many of the same activities, which made planning their future together quite easy. (They determined long ago that they were walking on the same path.) They decided to take a Spanish class at the local community college. They dazzled the younger students with their enthusiasm for learning. They joined a community orchestra and each learned to play a new instrument. They plan a trip and travel once every month or so. They cherish their grandchildren and spend a deliberately planned day with each of them as a birthday gift.

This couple carefully pondered and set goals for their retirement. They love each day and feel gratified as they reach each of their goals. I can say without a doubt that they will never say, "I wish I would have . . ."

Never regret that you didn't do something you had the power to do. Set your goals and rush to greet them.

SEVEN

# The Ultimate Guide for Your Life

When you set core, event, and continuation goals they serve as guides to assist you as you travel through life. If you have not seriously considered where you want your life to go, you will probably be dissatisfied with your life. This dissatisfaction can cause you to jump at every opportunity that comes along, hoping that a new situation will be the solution you seek.

In contrast, when your goals are in order, you are more likely to recognize the path you want when it comes along, thus it is easier to reach your destination. When your goals are not guiding you, you will try path after path, often never finding the one that is right for you. Goals are like having road signs that provide direction toward the path that you've determined is right for you.

Imagine that you are driving on a highway. You can always tell the drivers who know where they are going. They are not trying to make a left-hand turn from the right lane because they just realized they missed their street. They are not diverting their attention from the road ahead to read a map. They are not driving too slowly so they can read street signs hoping to see the name of the street they want. All of these things contribute to accidents involving those of us who know where we are going.

The same is true in life. We have all fallen victim to collisions with people who are driving without knowing where they are going. Collisions complicate lives. They are a burden to everyone involved, yet create the greatest nuisance for those of us who know where we are going because we actually have a plan and expect to arrive at our goals unscathed and in a timely fashion.

When you haven't set goals and go through life knowing only what you *don't* want, you jump at many paths hoping they will lead where you want to go. This is what I call *negative shopping*. It's like going into a grocery store with a list of what you don't want to buy. There are thousands of choices other than what is on your "don't buy" list. If you grab things off the shelves that are not on your list, you may or may not end up with items you like. The only thing you know for sure is that you don't have the items from your "don't buy" list. The risk in managing a shopping trip or your life in this manner is that you may end up wasting time and money and still have nothing that you really want.

I have a friend who is good at visualizing. She sometimes vividly visualizes what she doesn't want without visualizing what she does want, which has had some unexpected negative consequences. For example, she and her husband were unhappy with the conditions at his workplace. She continually visualized his job going away. Sure enough, it did. The company went bankrupt and her husband lost his job. Neither of them visualized the next step.

They didn't take time to visualize a job he would like to have and, as a result, he was without work for some time.

When you have thought through and visualized your core, event, and continuation goals, you know where you are headed when you wake up each morning. When you have visualized how your goals look, you will recognize them when you see them.

Whether you realize it or not, you make decisions every day. By virtue of the fact that you are able to make decisions, you are also able to be an active participant in setting goals. Each decision you make moves you closer to or farther from your goals. When you have a clear vision of your goals, it makes it easier for you to make decisions that move you toward them. It is better to not waste your time moving down a path when you can clearly see that it is not "your" path. It also makes it easier to realize when you are off-track.

Clearly define your goals and allow them to guide you each day.

# EIGHT

# Constructing Your Goal Book

You can purchase the items for your Goal Book individually or you can simply order the starter kit that is available on our website: www.ponderpictureprosper.com. The starter kit includes a three-ring binder, blank pages, and page protectors.

You will need the following to construct your Goal Book:

- A list of your goals
- A three-ring binder
- Paper on which to glue pictures
- Page protectors to hold the goal pages
- A glue stick

- Magazines, catalogs, travel brochures, free Internet sites, etc., that contain pictures that represent your goals (or you can draw your own pictures)
- Clarifying words or phrases that you have cut from other sources or ones you have written yourself
- Scissors to cut out your pictures and clarifying words
- Time to create the mood you want for each page

Visualize the mood you want in your life and create those images on each page of your Goal Book (put each goal on a single sheet of paper, not back to back, so you can change pages without disrupting the other side). Think of how you would like your life to look and feel. You may want to add words to the pages to help clarify your goals. Some people like to add sayings that they find meaningful. You can even add borders, stickers, and clip art. The most important aspect is that your Goal Book be a personal expression of the way you picture your goals.

Ponder your dreams, visualize them, and then create pages with words and pictures so you can prosper in life, love, and work.

## Goal Book Truths

- The universe brings what you need, when you need it, not necessarily when you want it. When you put a goal in your Goal Book, you should be ready for it to come to you and patient enough to wait.
- It is not useful to establish dates for your goals. The universe doesn't operate on deadlines. (I've tried sneaking in deadlines from time to time. Don't bother.)
- Do not expect to reach one goal a day or even once a month. Goals arrive when the time is right.
- Be sure you really want what you put in your Goal Book because you will most likely get it.

- You should consider your Goal Book to be a *goal catcher;* it helps you achieve what you want.
- You need to stretch yourself and continually set new goals—before you realize your current goals—otherwise you may flounder.
- It is not useful to put in outrageous things just to see if you can get them. A Goal Book is a serious exercise to determine what is important to you and what you truly want in life.
- Setting goals and placing them in a Goal Book is a way to focus your hope for their achievement. Think of it as *focused hope*.
- There are three kinds of goals: *core, event,* and *continuation*. Core goals are things such as happiness, health, love, joy, and prosperity. Event goals are things such as a wedding, the birth of a child, a new job, a new car, and a trip. Continuation goals are the elements of daily life, like a happy marriage, raising responsible children, and a satisfying job.
- Adjust your goals as your life changes. Don't try to set goals too far in advance.
- You cannot set goals for other people.
- Your Goal Book can't force the will of others. For example, you can't make a certain person give you something. You can't make a person marry you. You can't make someone quit smoking or drinking alcohol. You cannot impose your goals on others.
- You cannot set goals such as world peace. The goals in your Goal Book are for your life.
- If you have set conflicting goals for yourself, you won't get them at the same time.
- Don't limit your goals by what you think is likely to happen in your life. If you can visualize it, it can be.

Humans have never accomplished anything that they didn't first visualize.

- Keep dreaming and expecting the universe to work out the details.
- As goals are achieved, keep adding new goals to your Goal Book.
- Goals don't happen all at once. You can have some now and some later. Time is life's way of not having everything happen simultaneously. Be patient, you have a lifetime.
- If you have a goal that is illegal or immoral, you might *not* want to put it in the Goal Book because it will have serious consequences, even if the universe does work out the details!
- No matter how much you may want a goal, it can't defy the laws of nature.
- Maintain the attitude that your goals will be achieved.
- Goals are dreams with attitude.
- This is not an exact science, try and try again.

## Goal Book Management

- When your event goals are met, you can retire those pages to a section for goals that are achieved. If it is a travel destination where you would like to go again, you can update the page and leave it or just leave it as it is.
- Core goals should always remain a permanent part of your Goal Book.
- Continuation goals should be left in place as long as you want that condition in your life.
- As goals are met, add new pages. You continue to live and grow as a person. As you age, your goals change. Let your Goal Book grow with you. It can be a lifelong companion.

- Put your Goal Book in a prominent place where you can see your goals every day.
- It is important to look at your Goal Book often. If you are in a relationship and have shared goals with someone, look at the pages together. Talk about your goals. Talk about where you want to go and why.
- Feed your dreams and weave pictures of how you want your goals to look when they arrive. Every time you look at your goals, it nurtures them. It is like adding fertilizer to a garden. Soon you will be living your dreams.
- When you want to remind yourself of a specific goal, open your Goal Book to that page so you can see it every time you walk past.
- Set a time each year to generate new Goal Book pages. It's handy to set a regular time, like your birthday or New Year's Day, so you won't forget this important task.

Ponder and picture your goals. Make pages for each of them. And expect them to happen. When your goals are realized, they may not unfold exactly the way you envision. Accept what the universe brings you.

Ultimately your dreams, memories, and knowledge are the only things that can never be taken from you. My grandmother used to tell me to get all the education I could because it could never be taken away. Famine, fire, hurricane, death, war, and the other horrors of this world can't take away your dreams. You are the only enemy of your dreams. You are the only one who can choose to sacrifice them. Don't give them up without a fight or because you are afraid of prospering. Brush that fear aside, get some attitude, and then make your Goal Book.

Give yourself the opportunity to live happily ever after.

*Dream dreams, expect miracles, celebrate life,*
*and let the universe work out the details.*

# About the Author

Marsha Barber Clark has worked as a consultant, teacher, and director of non-profit organizations for more than twenty-five years. She has a Bachelor's degree in Education, a Master's degree in Marriage and Family Studies, and a Master's degree in Educational Administration.

Currently, she works as a motivational coach and speaker.

Marsha lives in Northern Michigan with her husband, Chuck. They have two adult sons, Brendan and Shane, who attend graduate school.

# What's Next?

Many people who have created Goal Books are already reaping the rewards of this process. As a result, Marsha is busy working on the sequel to this book—***Ponder Picture Prosper +***!

If you have a success story to share or a question about how to handle a particular situation while using a Goal Book and you would like to have it included in ***Ponder Picture Prosper +***, please submit your story or question using the "Contact Us" tab on the website www.ponderpictureprosper.com

## Guidelines for Submissions

Tell us about your success using a Goal Book. Include how you envisioned your goal in your book, details of how your goal was achieved, and how you felt when it was achieved. Please submit true unpublished success stories that have happened to you. Stories should be from 250-800 words. Please include contact information. Anonymous stories cannot be used. If your submission is accepted for publication you will be notified in advance.

Questions should be of general interest regarding Goal Book

construction, using a Goal Book within a family or work situation, clarification on specific aspects of Goal Book use, or other general concerns. If you have a specific question, you may submit it and it will be answered individually (as time allows) or in a group with similar questions on the website.

# Speaking & Workshops

An experienced speaker and presenter, Marsha Clark has inspired and delighted audiences of all ages from across the country. She is available to conduct workshops for your professional organization or private group and to speak at your next conference or seminar.

Marsha has coached and guided many individuals and families toward achieving their goals and living lives that more fully reflect their deepest desires. She would be delighted to speak at your next event.

Please contact Marsha at 231-377-2017 or www.ponderpictureprosper.com to discuss rates and references.

As one satisfied participant put it, "You're in for a treat!"

# Visit Our Website

To purchase additional copies of *Ponder Picture Prosper* and great Goal Book gear visit:

www.ponderpictureprosper.com.

If you want a special gift personalized by Marsha, please submit your request.

The website also features information on upcoming workshops, speaking engagements, and book signings; plus the answers to questions submitted by readers as they create their Goal Books.

Visit the site often for inspiring thoughts on how your Goal Book can help you create the life you have always wanted.